At Issue

Are America's Wealthy
Too Powerful?

Other books in the At Issue series:

At Issue

Are America's Wealthy Too Powerful?

Stuart A. Kallen, Book Editor

GREENHAVEN PRESS

An imprint of Thomson Gale, a part of The Thomson Corporation

THOMSON

™

GALE

Detroit • New York • San Francisco • San Diego • New Haven, Conn.
Waterville, Maine • London • Munich

Bonnie Szumski, *Publisher*
Helen Cothran, *Managing Editor*

© 2006 Thomson Gale, a part of The Thomson Corporation.

Thomson and Star Logo are trademarks and Gale and Greenhaven Press are registered trademarks used herein under license.

For more information, contact:
Greenhaven Press
27500 Drake Rd.
Farmington Hills, MI 48331-3535
Or you can visit our Internet site at http://www.gale.com

LIBRARY OF CONGRESS CATALOGING-IN-PUBLICATION DATA

Are America's Wealthy Too Powerful? / Stuart A. Kallen, book editor.
    p. cm. -- (At issue)
   Includes bibliographical references and index.
   ISBN 0-7377-3429-9 (lib. bdg. : alk. paper) ISBN 0-7377-3430-2 (pbk. : alk. paper)
  1. Wealth--Social aspects--United States. 2. Power (Social sciences)--United States. 3. Rich people--United States. 4. Corporations--Social aspects--United States. 5. Elite (Social sciences)--United States. 6. Equality--United States. I. Kallen, Stuart A., 1995– II. At issue (San Diego, Calif.)
   HC110.W4A73 2006
   339.20973--dc22
                                           2005054545

Printed in the United States of America
10 9 8 7 6 5 4 3 2 1

Contents

Introduction

The ideals of American democracy promise that all people, whatever their financial status, can influence the government by voting, running for office, or writing their representatives. However, there is a widespread perception that individuals and corporations with the most money have the greatest influence over elected politicians and the laws they write. According to a 2003 CBS poll, 60 percent of Americans believe that government policies favor the rich, 8 percent believe these policies help the middle class, and only 2 percent think they benefit the poor. These statistics suggest that a majority of Americans believe that the wealthy have too much power in America. On the other hand, many experts assert that all Americans have access to powerful means to influence politics in the United States.

Those who believe that the wealthy do indeed have too much power argue that the American electoral system allows the richest Americans to wield the most political influence. They point out that in 2004, political candidates running for the House, Senate, and the presidency collectively raised more than 1 billion dollars from wealthy supporters, defined as those who earn more than $230,000 annually. Although these affluent donors comprised 1 percent of the population, their contributions made up 70 percent of all the money donated to federal candidates—the rest came from unions, political action committees, and other interests. Critics of this system maintain that as long as politicians rely on campaign funds from the rich, legislative favors will be traded for money, an illegal activity known as quid pro quo, from the Latin for "equal exchange."

One piece of legislation that some argue is an example of quid pro quo is the Energy Act of 2005. In October 2004, after the Energy Act was approved by the Senate, the *Boston Globe* studied tens of thousands of pages of public records. These documents showed that those with business interests in energy policy contributed tens of millions of dollars to officials backing the legislation. According to the *Globe*:

> [Analysis] shows that the corporations and others . . . were rewarded in the bill with tax breaks, construction projects, and easements of regulations that would save them much more than they spent making their arguments to the government. . . . The nuclear industry, which spent some $71,405,955 [on] Capitol Hill, would get $7.37 billion in tax breaks and projects, including federal funds to construct a $1 billion nuclear plant in Idaho.

Mark Longabaugh, senior vice president for public affairs for the League of Conservation Voters commented, "What's really amazing is how a combination of energy industry, oil and gas industry, utility industry guys, coal industry guys . . . literally got billions of dollars in payback for millions of dollars in contributions."

Those who do not believe that the wealthy are too powerful argue that average American citizens have an influential political voice. They note that middle class Americans who currently earn between $25,000 and $90,000 a year—60 percent of the U.S. adult population—enjoy numerous government entitlements. Many of these benefits, such as Social Security and the mortgage interest tax deduction, are sacrosanct in American politics. An example of the power that average Americans wield over Congress may be seen in the debate over changing the Social Security system. This retirement program, funded through a dedicated payroll tax, paid out almost $500 billion in benefits in 2004. In January 2005, President George W. Bush described the Social Security system as "headed for bankruptcy" and proposed partially privatizing the program by allowing workers to invest a percentage of their payroll taxes in the stock market. Critics argued that such a change would provide billions in profits to wealthy Wall Street financial firms.

As the debate ensued, thousands of Americans contacted their representatives and the White House via phone calls, e-mails, and letters to protest changes in the program. Their political clout was multiplied by AARP (formerly known as the American Association of Retired Persons), whose 35 million members make up a broad cross section of working- and middle-class Americans aged fifty or older. Taking center stage in the debate, AARP spent more than $5 million on television ads attacking Bush's Social Security plan. In addition, the organization dispatched volunteers to protest at town hall meetings held by congressional representatives who supported the plan.

With a huge member base and an $800 million annual budget, AARP had a major influence on the debate. As the *Washington Post* noted in March 2005, "Both its friends and adversaries agree: AARP holds the key to how or whether Social Security will be restructured this year. . . . [Polls] show that a majority of voters reject Bush's plan to make investment accounts part of the retirement program, a result that can be attributed in part to AARP's persuasiveness."

With membership dues of only $12.50 a year, AARP provides an influential collective voice to average Americans. Some argue that this kind of influence far exceeds the power of the rich to influence legislation and that there are thousands of such associations and grassroots organizations that provide access to power to any Americans who care to take part in the political debate. In short, they assert, it is a myth that the wealthy have the preponderance of power in America because the U.S. political system offers multiple avenues for people to express their opinions and influence legislation.

The debate over money, politics, influence, and fairness has been ongoing since the founding of the United States and clearly will continue in the coming years. In *At Issue: Are America's Wealthy Too Powerful?* the authors present a variety of perspectives about this perennial controversy in America.

1

The Wealthy Profit at the Expense of the Poor and Middle Classes

James Lardner

James Lardner is director and founder of Inequality.org, an organization founded to illuminate the causes and consequences of what he considers America's growing concentration of wealth and power in the hands of fewer people. Lardner's articles have appeared in the New Yorker, *the* New York Review of Books, *and the* Washington Post. *He is the coauthor of* NYPD: A City and Its Police.

There is little doubt that the rich are getting richer at the expense of the poor and middle class. Studies show that CEO salaries have risen an astronomical 2,500 percent and that the 13,000 richest families have a combined income that is nearly equal to the income of America's 20 million poorest families. Until the 1970s a majority of Americans would have expressed outrage at this inequality. However, in recent years, a propaganda campaign to convince people that there is nothing wrong with this disgraceful inequality has been waged by corporate officials and the politicians who serve them. Unless citizens step up to take control from corporations and denounce the great income disparity, democracy will become meaningless in the United States.

On October 20th [2003], barely a week after the House and Senate agreed to let the Bush administration have its way with Iraq and Saddam Hussein, the *New York Times Magazine* ran a cover story entitled "The End of Middle-Class America (and the Triumph of the Plutocrats)." It was the longest, strongest, and most forthright article on the subject to appear in any major magazine or newspaper to date. When the preoccupation with foreign enemies fades—if it ever does—the *Times*'s decision to publish such a story may be remembered as a watershed moment.

"The 13,000 richest families in America" had "incomes 300 times that of average families," or . . . "almost as much income as the 20 million poorest households."

In his 8000-word jeremiad, *Times* columnist (and Princeton University professor) Paul Krugman makes quick work of the various reassuring counter-arguments that most mainstream publications have felt obliged to consider at length. Citing a [2003] . . . study by Thomas Piketty of the French research institute Cepremap and Emmanuel Saez of the University of California at Berkeley, Krugman points out that in 1998 the top .01 percent of taxpayers collected more than 3 percent of Americans' total income (up from .7 percent of total income in 1970). In other words, "the 13,000 richest families in America" had "incomes 300 times that of average families," or, in absolute terms, "almost as much income as the 20 million poorest households."

"All indications are that the explosion of incomes at the top continued through 2000," Krugman writes. While "the plunge in stock prices must have put some crimp in high incomes," census data shows the gulf widening in 2001, "mainly because of the severe effects of the recession on the working poor and near poor." It's a safe bet, Krugman adds, that . . . "we will find ourselves a society in which income inequality is even higher than it was in the late 90's."

America is often described as the world's richest nation. It might be more accurate to say we have the world's richest rich people. Set them aside, and, as Krugman observes, "Swedish living standards are way ahead of those in the U.S. Swedish families with children that are at the 10th percentile—poorer than 90 percent of the population—have incomes 60 percent higher than their U.S. counterparts. And very few people in Sweden experience the deep poverty that is all too common in the United States. One measure: in 1994 only 6 percent of Swedes lived on less than $11 per day, compared with 14 percent in the U.S."

On a recent [2003] "Crossfire," conservative commentator Robert Novak raked a Canadian viewer over the coals for daring to suggest that Canadians live longer than Americans do. "Marg, like most Canadians, you're ill informed and wrong," Novak told her. "The U.S. has the longest standard of living— longest life expectancy of any country in the world, including Canada. That's the truth."

"But it was Novak who had his facts wrong," Krugman points out. "Canadians can expect to live about two years longer than Americans. In fact, life expectancy in the U.S. is well below that in Canada, Japan and every major nation in Western Europe. On average, we can expect lives a bit shorter than those of Greeks, a bit longer than those of Portuguese. Male life expectancy is lower in the U.S. than it is in Costa Rica."

A Campaign to Cloud the Facts

Such forthrightness is rare. So is Krugman's conclusion about why income and wealth have become so much more concentrated in the past two-plus decades. Not just because of increased global competition or the shift toward occupations in which only a few have the necessary skills. . . . Not, in Krugman's view, because of any of the various irresistible economic forces cited by so many of the academics and Think Tankers who have written on these matters. "Globalization can explain part of the relative decline in blue-collar wages, but it can't explain the 2,500 percent rise in C.E.O. incomes," he argues. "Technology may explain why the salary premium associated with a college education has risen, but it's hard to match up with the huge increase in inequality among the college-educated, with little progress for many but gigantic gains at the top. The superstar theory works for [*Tonight Show* star] Jay Leno, but not for the thousands of people who have become awesomely rich without going on TV."

At bottom, we may be talking not so much about an economic shift as about a cultural one—the erosion of a national consensus that kept high incomes in check from the 1940s into the 1970s. Since then, according to Krugman, there's been a drastic reduction in the self-restraint of those at the top, made possible by a great wave of acquiescence on the part of those on the bottom or in what remains of the middle. What accounts for the acquiescence? The biggest factor, Krugman suggests, may be the relentless efforts of the wealthy and their ideological allies to bring it about.

Study upon study has sought to minimize or refute the evidence of increased inequality. But the question would be beyond debate, in Krugman's view, if it weren't for a well-funded campaign to cloud the facts. A generation ago, skeptics could reasonably claim that the inequality of income and wealth wasn't a huge issue for the U.S., because the absolute amount of wealth in the hands of the ulta-rich wasn't a significant share of the whole. That's no longer true. "These days 1 percent of families receive about 16 percent of total pretax income, and have about 14 percent of after-tax income," Krugman notes. "That share has roughly doubled over the past 30 years, and is now about as large as the share of the bottom 40 percent of the population." That shift alone has made a major contribution to the stagnating and declining economic fortunes of a large part of the population.

At this point, he argues, the nay-saying should be understood less as a serious intellectual position than as a "sizable, well-financed industry . . . itself a symptom of the growing influence of our emerging plutocracy."

The Outrage Is Gone

CEO pay—often treated as a phenomenon unto itself—is merely the larger story in microcosm, according to Krugman. "For a generation after World War II, fear of outrage kept executive salaries in check," he writes. "Now the outrage is gone. That is, the explosion of executive pay represents a social change rather than the purely economic forces of supply and demand. We should think of it not as a market trend like the rising value of waterfront property, but as something more like the sexual revolution of the 1960s—a relaxation of old strictures, a new permissiveness." In the 1960s, he notes, [economist] John Kenneth Galbraith described the honest executive as one who "eschews the lovely, available and even naked women by whom he is intimately surrounded." Now, Krugman adds, the attitude of most executives is: "If it feels good, do it."

The explosion of executive pay represents a social change rather than the purely economic forces of supply and demand.

With office-holders ever more dependent on the financial support of the most fortunate Americans, a whole new reality has taken hold of the leaders and institutions that might, under other circumstances, be working to resist the inequality tide. As an example, Krugman cites the recent to-do in Washington over a proposal to crack down on "tax exiles"—those who renounce their citizenship to avoid U.S. taxes. Texas Senator Phil Gramm denounced the idea of penalizing such people as a proposal "right out of Nazi Germany." Another piece of legislation to the same effect was described by Daniel Mitchell of the Heritage Foundation (writing in the *Washington Times*) as the "Dred Scott tax bill"—as if the liberty of Americans fleeing taxation today deserves protection as much as the liberty of the escaped slaves of the 1850s.

"We live in extreme times," Krugman writes. "Even if the forms of democracy remain, they may become meaningless. It's all too easy to see how we may become a country in which the big rewards are reserved for people with the right connections; in which ordinary people see little hope of advancement; in which political involvement seems pointless, because in the end the interests of the elite always get served.

"It's all too easy to see how we may become a country in which the big rewards are reserved for people with the right connections; in which ordinary people see little hope of advancement."

"Am I being too pessimistic? Even my liberal friends tell me not to worry, that our system has great resilience, that the center will hold. I hope they're right, but they may be looking in the rearview mirror. Our optimism about America, our belief that in the end our nation always finds its way, comes from the past—a past in which we were a middle-class society."

2

The Wealthy Create Opportunities and Jobs for All Americans

Donald Luskin

Donald Luskin is chief investment officer of Trend Macrolytics LLC, an economics and investment research firm.

During the past two decades the U.S. economy has undergone a positive transformation thanks to free trade, new business invest-ment, and the digital revolution. Although these powerful finan-cial forces have brought benefits to nearly all Americans, the economy has also made some individuals incredibly rich. While this has created economic disparity between the super rich and the rest of society, the phenomenon is nothing new. Whenever a booming economy creates great opportunity, some do well while others fall behind. Despite long-winded articles in the Wall Street Journal *and the* New York Times *decrying the perceived widening of income disparity, almost all Americans are better off than they were in the 1960s. Although liberals continue to bash the rich, most Americans believe that this is a land of equal op-portunity where anyone with talent and intelligence can make a fortune. Those who control the powerful media ignore Americans' optimism that they will be able to get ahead in life.*

Starting on May 13 [2005], the *Wall Street Journal* ran a se-ries of four-page stories—totaling almost 10,000 words—

about what it manifestly considered a major threat to the Republic. Two days later, the *New York Times* launched a series of a dozen stories about the same threat, most of the articles splashed on page one, above the fold: a total of nearly 50,000 words. *BusinessWeek,* the *Christian Science Monitor,* and the *Los Angeles Times* have taken up the story, too; Michael Kinsley, writing in the *L.A. Times,* even suggested that the *Washington Post* get into the act.

Was the furor about al-Qaeda? Iran? North Korean nukes? Nope. The sword of Damocles hanging over our national future—and discovered, coincidentally, by all of these mainstream liberal media outlets at once—is . . . income inequality. But a concerned citizen who wades through these tens of thousands of words, and pores over the studies they solemnly cite as authoritative, will find a simple, but highly reassuring, truth: There's no story here.

The *Journal* and the *Times* are exercised by reports that, over the last three decades, a new class of what the *Times* calls the "hyper-rich" has arisen in the United States, resulting in a disparity in incomes between rich and poor not seen since the 1920s: the most severe income inequality in the developed world today. How did this happen? As the *Times,* explains it, "The hyper-rich have emerged . . . as the biggest winners in a remarkable transformation of the American economy characterized by, among other things, the creation of a more global marketplace, new technology and investment spurred partly by tax cuts."

Extremely Wealthy Individuals

Fair enough. We have indeed seen a transformative era of economic growth. That era has indeed produced a whole new class of extremely wealthy individuals—or, more accurately, a whole new class of individuals became extremely wealthy as their reward for taking the risks that made that growth happen. And indeed tax cuts were at the root of it—supply-side tax cuts that increased the incentives for risk-taking in the first place.

But none of this is exactly man-bites-dog material. What the *Times* reports as news is a pattern that should be familiar to economic historians: Times of great prosperity have been associated with greater income inequality (for example, the 1920s), and conversely times of economic decline have been associated with greater equality (the 1930s). The lines of causality here are complex, and no doubt run in both directions: Prosperity is both the cause and the effect of inequality, and decline is both the cause and the effect of equality. So ideological advocates of income equality for its own sake ought to be careful what they wish for.

The fact remains that income has risen for all: The rising tide has lifted all boats.

The great prosperity of the last three decades has been dominated by American technological and commercial prowess. So no one should be surprised that the emergence of the new hyper-rich has been preeminently an American phenomenon. Today 341 of the world's 691 billionaires—including five of the top ten—are Americans. These aren't old-money names, either. You have to get all the way down to number 243 before you find a Rockefeller. At the top of the chart are Gates, Buffett, Ellison, Allen, Walton—precisely the people whose innovations and risk-taking made our current prosperity possible. Much of the rise in American income inequality could probably be erased in one fell swoop just by getting these 341 people to move to another country.

We need to focus, then, on the question: What harm has it done to have this new class of the hyper-rich on the American scene? The *Times* and the *Journal* both go on at length about how Americans who used to consider themselves very rich— one thinks inevitably of the Sulzbergers of the *Times*, and the

Bancrofts of Dow Jones—are rather annoyed to have to compete society with the new hyper-rich; old money has never liked new money. But in truth, the incomes of the hyper-rich have not come at the expense of anyone else. The poverty rate, for example, hasn't risen over the last 30 years; it has actually fallen slightly. Average after-tax, inflation-adjusted income has risen for every income quintile in the population. Yes, it has risen the most for the highest quintile, and risen the least for the lowest—but this can be explained to some extent by the great wave of immigration over the same period. The fact remains that income has risen for all: The rising tide has lifted all boats.

Three Cheers for Diversity

Before the present era of transformative growth and its concomitant income inequality, many economists had expected the mid-20th-century trend toward greater equality to persist forever. According to the influential hypothesis of [economist] Simon Kuznets, nearly a half-century of steadily rising equality of income following the technology revolution that peaked in the 1920s was explained by the fact that more and more workers were joining the high-productivity sectors of the economy. Now it appears that what Kuznets described may be, in fact, a cyclical phenomenon that restarted at some point about 25 years ago. Economists Emmanuel Saez and Thomas Piketty have written that "a new industrial revolution has taken place, thereby leading to increasing inequality, and inequality will decline again at some point, as more and more workers benefit from the innovations."

In other words, at the beginning of each cycle a small band of risk-takers get extremely wealthy in the vanguard of economic transformation, but that's only a one-time effect. For years afterward, everyone else in the economy adapts to the new, higher productivity potential that the new rich have made possible, and incomes gradually gravitate toward greater equality. Happily, then, those who hope for greater income equality need not wish for slower growth, or for the mass deportation of our billionaires. All that is required is patience—and hard work.

"A new industrial revolution has taken place, thereby leading to increasing inequality, and inequality will decline again at some point, as more and more workers benefit from the innovations."

But income inequality will never go away entirely—and it's not at all clear that we should want it to. Even if a socialist-minded fairy godmother were to wave her magic wand and set all incomes to perfect equality, in a free economy they would immediately drift toward inequality owing entirely to voluntary choices made by each individual. Each of us would choose freely whether to work hard or take it easy; to marry a working spouse or a stay-at-home; to educate ourselves for a better job, or settle for less; to invest in income-producing securities or just spend our money. All these things would determine our unequal incomes, just as they do today. To be sure, in the real world we don't make those choices from an initial position of equality. Some of us are born rich, others poor, most in between. Nevertheless it's choices like these that determine whether we will rise or fall within the class in which we are born, or move upward or downward to another class. So we shouldn't fear income inequality: We should celebrate it as "income diversity."

Income Mobility

Changing our incomes by making choices different from those of our parents is called "income mobility." Both the *Wall Street Journal* and the *New York Times* correctly acknowledge this practice as fundamental to American life (and both happen to discuss Benjamin Franklin as its exemplar). Yet the papers argue that income mobility is on the decline just as income inequality is on the rise. You'd think that the emergence of a whole new class of the hyper-rich would prove that income mobility is alive and well (they had to come from somewhere, after all). But no.

The *Times* and the *Journal* cite many authoritative-sounding studies on declining income mobility. But to get an accurate picture, you'd have to track hundreds of millions of individuals through time, monitoring changes across generations in such factors as income, tax rates, wealth, lifestyle, and education. Looking back further than a couple of decades, robust statistics are hard to find in standard databases; you can't ask all the individuals concerned, because many of them are deceased. So researchers end up relying on surveys of small samples of people, containing what they can recollect about their parents' and grandparents' economic circumstances. As a result, hard facts about economic mobility are elusive, and studies about it are approximate and subjective at best.

Yet for all that, the *Times* and *Journal* stories are peppered with definitive-sounding statements, like this one from the *Times:* "One study, by the Federal Reserve Bank of Boston, found that fewer families moved from one quintile, or fifth, of the income ladder to another during the 1980s than during the 1970s and that still fewer moved in the 90s than in the 80s." If you follow the *Times*'s link to this study, it turns out actually to be about women in the workforce and what happens to families when a spouse dies; the more general findings cited by the *Times* are buried in an appendix. Yes, that appendix shows that about 4 percent more households stayed in their income quintile during the 1990s than in the 1970s. But it also shows—though the *Times* doesn't mention this—that in the 1990s more households than ever jumped from the poorest quantile to the richest. But none of this is reliable anyway: A footnote reveals that the statistics are derived from the Panel Study of Income Dynamics database, an ongoing survey that tracks only 8,000 families out of a U.S. population of 295 million individuals.

The other studies cited are based on evidence equally unreliable, and come to conclusions even less interesting. At most, these surveys suggest that—maybe—income mobility has stopped improving over the last 30 years.

Perhaps the best research method for getting our arms around the slippery topic of income mobility is simply to take a poll, and ask people how they feel about it. The *New York Times* itself took such a poll, and its optimistic results are strikingly at odds with the paper's gloomy conclusions. Eighty percent of respondents said "it's still possible to start out poor in this country, work hard, and become rich"—up from 57 percent in 1983. Twenty-five percent said they believed their children's standard of living would be "much better" than their own—up from 18 percent in 1994. Forty-six percent said hard work is "essential" for getting ahead in life—up from 36 percent in 1987.

Resenting Prosperity

So where's the beef? Everyone's gotten richer—and a few have gotten hyper-rich. And there's no real reason to think that income mobility isn't alive and well. So why this full-court press by the liberal mainstream media to create the impression that America is becoming a feudal society? Maybe it's a media thing; there's no other industry more obsessed with pigeonholing people by class. Here, for example, is how the *New York Times* sees its readers: They're "nearly three times as likely as the average U.S. adult to have a college or post-graduate degree, more than twice as likely to be a professional/managerial and more than twice as likely to have a household income exceeding $100,000."

Or maybe it's a liberal thing. You're more likely to vote Democratic if you're convinced that "the rich" are keeping you from getting your fair share—you know, "Two Americas" and all that. And you're more likely to support liberal initiatives like affirmative action if you think that the American dream based on income mobility is falling apart. So liberal media outlets such as the *Times* go through periodic frenzies about income inequality, regardless of who's in the White House. (Two typical *Times* headlines, from 1998: "In Booming Economy, Poor Still Struggle to Pay the Rent" and "Benefits Dwindle for the Unskilled Along with Wages.")

For the liberal media, demonizing the rich is a powerful way to fight against those conservative initiatives.

And, of course, the putative problem of income inequality is yet another opportunity for the liberal media to excoriate the Bush tax cuts. Whatever the problem—Social Security solvency, economic growth, outsourcing to China, budget deficits—repealing those tax cuts is always the liberal answer. In this case, the *Times* claims they "stand to widen the gap between the hyper-rich and the rest of America." This year [2005] Congress will vote on the extension of President Bush's tax cuts on income from dividends and capital gains, and on making permanent the repeal of the estate tax. For the liberal media, demonizing the rich is a powerful way to fight against those conservative initiatives. There's good reason, though, to think it won't work. That *Times* poll that showed how much faith Americans have in their income mobility also produced a striking result about taxes on "the rich": Seventy-six percent of respondents said they opposed the estate tax.

3

Wall Street Financiers Manipulate the Stock Market to Benefit Themselves

Ian Williams

Ian Williams is the UN correspondent for Nation *magazine. He writes frequently for* AlterNet, Foreign Policy in Focus, *and* Salon.

Millions of Americans put their savings in pension plans and mutual funds. However, the finance industry exists largely to benefit a few wealthy insiders, such as brokers, bankers, and corporate CEOs, who seem to make money whether the market goes up or down. By charging exorbitant fees, devising scams, and falsifying financial information, this elite group earns billions of dollars at the expense of average investors. With steadily eroding government oversight and regulation, the stock market has become a place where scam artists, masquerading as brokers, exist to serve only themselves and their corporate bosses.

Every year, ordinary Americans put billions, indeed trillions of dollars into Wall Street. Even if we do not directly own a single share, our pension funds and our insurance companies pour our money into the financial markets that are, as we are often told, the secret of our success as the world's largest economy.

Adam Smith, the father of modern economics much-quoted by conservatives, once said, "People of the same trade seldom meet together, even for merriment and diversion, but the conversation ends in a conspiracy against the public, or in some contrivance to raise prices." It's a description that fits today's Wall Street to a tee.

They may not be the evil capitalists favored by those Soviet cartoons of yore, sitting in smoke-filled rooms in their top hats. They may not be scheming to take over the world, as some in the anti-globalization movement would have you believe. But the current workings of the finance industry are, in sum, a giant conspiracy to loot ordinary investors for the benefit of its members and their friends.

> *The current workings of the finance industry are, in sum, a giant conspiracy to loot ordinary investors for the benefit of its members and their friends.*

The sources for my paranoia on this point are not loony Leninists, but the financial sections of major newspapers. The *Wall Street Journal* and the *Financial Times* look increasingly like a cross between the *National Inquirer* and a criminal court docket, with Captains of Finance pictured daily doing a perp walk across their pages [after being arrested].

While adding the throwaway caveat that there are many sincere and honest people in the finance sector, we should note that in order to stay honest, they almost have to buck the system. To prove my point, let's trace the progress of your hard-earned dollars through the financial food chain.

Funds Tied to Brokers' Interests

Let's say an unwitting investor goes to a broker, who then recommends a mutual fund. Hitherto regarded as unassailable, the mutual fund's virtue is now under question thanks to the investigation launched by New York's attorney general Eliot Spitzer [in November 2003]. To begin with, your broker may be receiving kickbacks from the fund managers for steering you in the "right" direction. So your money is going to the fund that gives the broker the best returns rather than you.

To add insult to the proverbial injury, not all investors are made equal in the eyes of a mutual fund. They often offer special deals to major investors, who are allowed to trade after the markets have officially closed for the day. It's a bit like allowing people to bet on a horse race after the winners have gone past the finishing post.

The funds are also tied to the brokers' interests in other ways. The "sell-side" of brokerage firms is made up not just of stock sales teams, but also of analysts. These so-called independent researchers recommend which companies to buy—always an overwhelming majority of those on offer—and which to sell, a number that is all too frighteningly small.

There is usually a strong correlation between "buy" recommendations and whether or not the brokerage house has a stake in the contract for new stock issues—or hopes to acquire one in the future. While analysts are supposed to be protected by a "Chinese Wall" from such temptations, bonuses and commissions often make up a large part of their remuneration. I have spoken to several who confess to netting $100,000 for making one phone call.

Many mutual funds took a beating . . . [between 2001 and 2003] because they followed the sell-side analysts' recommendations and pumped their money into the bubble stocks that were being touted by the brokers and bankers. It is the average investor, however, who paid for their abysmal performance. The mutuals either took a percentage of your money up front, or charged you a management fee for losing your money.

Here are your choices then. Invest in a mutual fund or invest in the companies recommended by your broker—and in either case end up as a victim of the same bad advice.

A Chain of Sticky Hands

However you invest your hard-earned money, it is likely to go through the New York Stock Exchange [NYSE]. Unlike the NASDAQ [stock exchange], the NYSE has a network of so-called "specialists," who act as middlemen between buyers and sellers. It now turns out that these firms were skimming off the top themselves. Instead of matching the seller with a potential buyer, the specialists bought the stock themselves and resold it to the seller at a slight profit. But don't worry, the Exchange regulates itself, which is why the directors hand-picked by former Chairman Richard Grasso paid him a whopping $180 million for putting them on the regulatory board.

After passing through this chain of sticky hands, at last your money arrives at its destination, ready to do its job, i.e. finance the American economy. And does it? Well, yes, but only up to a point.

A bulk of [Initial Public Offering] stocks were sold not to the public, but to friends, management, potential clients, and the executives of the company.

If you invested in an Initial Public Offering [IPO] at the height of the dot.com boom, for example, a large chunk of your money (around 20 percent) went in charges and fees to bankers, lawyers and the finance houses that pulled together the deal. Of course, you'd have to wait your turn for that privilege. A bulk of IPO stocks were sold not to the public, but to friends, management, potential clients, and the executives of the company, who got their stock allocations at the beginning, along with the big institutional investors.

These good Samaritans then collectively pumped the stock until it reached dizzying heights, and then unloaded it to individual stock holders mesmerized by the tales of fools' gold available in IPO's—i.e. you. You were left watching it reconnect with the laws of gravity, as it hit rock bottom with a leaden thump.

Herein lies the telltale evidence of Wall Street greed. If the IPO's were about raising money for the company, then those involved would clearly want to get the highest price for the stock the moment it went on the market. But if the entire process was intended instead as a scam to loot the public, using the company as bait, then it makes sense to charge the lowest price at the outset to a select group of people who can then make a huge profit when the stock price soars.

CEOs Make a Killing on Stock Options

Unfortunately, even if the shares don't immediately sink like a stone, your money isn't particularly safe. The CEOs of this world get much of their atrociously over-inflated rewards not from salary, but from options to buy shares. Stock options are supposed to "incentivize" managements to work harder. (Why we expect so many Americans to be inspired to feats of productivity just by a minimum wage, while others should need untold millions to give their best, is another story.) While the motivational effects of options are at best suspect, they do provide an incentive to hype the price of the shares so that high-level management can clean up. [The financial scandals at] Enron, Tyco, WorldCom, Global Crossing, Arthur Anderson, should all ring an alarm bell or two.

Corporate executives of such companies do not like paying dividends, because that goes to the ordinary shareholders. Instead they extol the virtues of "shareholder value," of increasing the stock price. Indeed, many of them tell their shareholders that rather than "waste" money paying out dividends—which until the . . . [2003] Bush giveaway [corporate tax cuts] was taxable—they prefer to buy back stock for the company to raise the share price.

There are several holes in this argument. One is that most ordinary shareholders own shares through their pension plans, and do not pay tax on dividends. The second is the uncanny similarity between the number of shares "bought back" by the company and the number of options issued to high-ranking company executives. In other words, under the banner of shareholder value, shareholders and employees are being once again robbed. Think of all those Enron employees whose pensions were locked up in plummeting stock, even as the executives were dumping their shares.

Ignoring Abuses

The moral, of course, is that free markets be damned, if people can make off with your money, you can be damn sure that they will—unless someone stops them. We have the best regulators in the world, of course. The NYSE checks the listings; the SEC [Securities and Exchange Commission] monitors the company filings; independent auditors keep tabs on the books; and a board elected by the shareholders scrutinizes the company strategy. All of these men and women, each dedicated to a single end: the welfare of the shareholders. Right?

> *If people can make off with your money, you can be damn sure that they will.*

Let's see. The National Association of Securities Dealers keeps most of its judgments against its member's secret, so you have no idea if the nice broker trying to sell you a parcel of Enron has a "record." The New York Stock Exchange is part of the problem and not the solution, as its new chairman John Reed has tacitly admitted. The Securities and Exchange Commission, on the admission of its previous chairman, was lobbied into not counting the cost of stock options to managements as part of doing business. Besides, even if the lobbyists allowed it to work harder, it is already far too overstretched to mind the coop.

Most of its judgments are arrived at through mutual consent. So if a corporate honcho steals millions of dollars, he will avoid prison time and indeed a criminal record as long as he repays a little bit of it. Indeed, he will probably be invited to the White House and made a member of the president's inner-circle of "friends" if he makes a big enough donation with his loot. On the other hand, try stealing a few knick-knacks from a Wal-Mart and see where that will get you!

With the financial regulators displaying such fine form, we're left with [New York attorney general] Elliot Spitzer and other state attorney generals, who may have political ambitions, but are doing a better job of fighting these large-scale forms of white-collar crime. Thanks to them, Wall Street may try and genuinely clean up its act—for the moment.

However, the Street is based on the lemming principle. Much of this self-flagellation only happened when the market tanked. That was when the ponzi schemes unraveled and the truth about the rosy corporate accounting dawned on investors.

The next time the market goes up, you can bet that they will all be at it again. The same institutions will join in on the feeding frenzy, persuading average Joes and Janes to put their savings in the hands of this great money-skimming machine.

Wall Street Financiers Help Millions of Investors Profit

Karl Zinsmeister

Karl Zinsmeister has been editor in chief of the American Enterprise *magazine since 1994. He has traveled three times to Iraq
as an embedded journalist, and writes about current affairs, social and economic trends, and cultural issues.*

*Wall Street has played a major role in making America one of
the most prosperous nations on earth. By attracting the best and
brightest financial minds from across the globe, the financial sector has revolutionized trading, banking, and personal finance.
Because of the efforts of financiers, Americans have easy access to
unique investment options, low-interest mortgages, and start-up
business capital. Although some major Wall Street players have
been embroiled in scandal, the large majority are honest and
keep the economy running efficiently. Wall Street brokers deserve
recognition for offering investment opportunities and improving
the lives of rich, middle-class, and poor people.*

You can love or loathe Wall Street and the whole machin-
ery of investment capitalism. Both passions have deep
American roots. But the reality is, every person living in the
U.S. is heavily indebted to the traders, bankers, and brokers
who fund our business start-ups, fill our retirement accounts,
finance our factories and buildings, and keep our economy
balanced and humming. If you have a mortgage, work at a

corporation, save money for college, or buy the products of a new company, you are a beneficiary of America's super-efficient, hyper-creative financial sector.

Every person living in the U.S. is heavily indebted to the traders, bankers, and brokers who fund our business start-ups, fill our retirement accounts . . . and keep our economy balanced and humming.

Even if you are living on charity, you are indebted to Wall Street—perhaps more than anyone. Thanks in considerable measure to investment growth, the total net worth of Americans rocketed from $7 trillion in 1950 to close to $40 trillion today (in constant dollars), and much of this increase is being channeled into philanthropy. An estimated $34 trillion will be given away over the next generation by successful investors. Those donations will build schools, cure diseases, erect museums, and underwrite social rejuvenations of all sorts. If you think that high finance benefits only fat cats, try living in a non-investing society. They are not good places for little people.

American financiers live and breathe to extend the profitability of businesses, and that is no small task. As even arch-unionist Samuel Gompers, the first president of the American Federation of Labor, recognized: The worst crime against working people is a company that fails to make a profit—for that company will not long remain an employer, or supplier, or buyer of other workers' goods.

Most Americans appreciate all this, and do not need to be convinced of the importance of private investment. Much more than other nationalities, Americans are thoroughly enmeshed in investing and small-scale capitalism; about half of all adults now own stocks or bonds. In Germany, only 10 percent do. According to Merrill Lynch's annual survey, 24 per-

cent of U.S. *teenagers* now own stock, so our habits of investing will only deepen as generations age.

There is no other country in the world that has capital markets as large and healthy as ours. The total value of U.S. stock came to 114 percent of our gross domestic product in 1996. The corresponding figure was 66 percent in Japan, 38 percent in France, and just 28 percent in Germany, reports economics writer Brink Lindsey. These vast stock accumulations, and the fact that our markets are more trustworthy and efficient than others, leave everyone from sheiks in Bahrain to industrial titans in South Korea hankering to place their money alongside our own in American investments. This fuels U.S. businesses, makes the dollar the world's favorite currency, and gives us an historically unprecedented level of affluence and economic security.

Americans are thoroughly enmeshed in investing and small-scale capitalism; about half of all adults now own stocks or bonds.

This U.S. advantage is widening. A couple of decades ago, London, Tokyo, and Germany challenged New York as centers of world finance. Today, all three of those rivals have been decisively surpassed, especially the latter two. In Japan, firms like Goldman Sachs, Merrill Lynch, and Morgan Stanley now dominate investment banking. London is a powerful money center, but in terms of investing volume and innovative ways of raising and applying capital, it lags U.S. markets. Economist Lawrence Kudlow characterizes Wall Street's current advantage over its competitors as "insurmountable."

Wall Street Intellectuals

One of the reasons our financial sector has grown so potent is because it has drawn heavily on America's best minds. Over the last generation, we have seen an intellectualization of investing; in particular, math and science have met Wall Street in a big way. In his forthcoming book on the stock market, AEI [American Enterprise Institute] economist Kevin Hassett touches on some of the new quantitative techniques money managers use to uncover market discontinuities, and notes that many of the innovators are not people trained in finance or business, but rather extremely bright refugees from fields like theoretical physics, psychology, biology, computer science, and mathematics.

Bruce Kovner, who serves on the American Enterprise Institute's board of trustees, is a quiet, modest man who will probably be annoyed to have me draw attention to him, but he is a perfect model of the new Wall Street intellectual, and what these individuals have added to our finance world. Twenty-five years ago, Kovner was a star Ph.D. student of Harvard political scientist Edward Banfield, and an enthusiastic harpsichordist and budding collector of rare books. Then, amidst a fit of writer's block while working on his dissertation, he borrowed $3,000 to start trading copper and other commodities. He turned out to have a gift for the work. Over the last decade, he has been America's most successful hedge-fund manager, employing Russian-émigré mathematicians and other such whizzes to help him execute his arcane trades, and generating literally billions of dollars of profits in the process. . . .

As stock market historian B. Mark Smith told me . . . "The investment business has become much more sophisticated. Even ten years ago, firms took huge risks using little more than seat-of-the-pants intuition. Today's new quantitative techniques have dramatically lowered the risk profiles." Just the same, superlative investing remains an art, and even in an era of heavy financial engineering and cookie-cutter systemization of trading, the great talents able to spot opportunities invisible to others will, almost by definition, have a rare sixth sense.

This was clear to me when I recently met a friend who had worked on Capitol Hill at the same time I did. "Bud" shifted gears after a few years and embarked to Wall Street, where he quickly became a legendary trader. Just weeks before we talked, he made millions of dollars for his firm by anticipating the demise of Enron [Corporation]—and he did so in the most un-high-tech way imaginable. The reported profit levels of the energy trading industry simply smelled improbably high to him a year or two ago. At that point he wasn't looking at Enron in particular, but rather at the broader industry Enron occupied with several other companies. Working backwards from the claimed profitability of these firms, using very simple math, he quickly realized that the scope of the business could not explicably produce such aggregate earnings. Without a whiff of the specific finagling then going on at Enron, he knew someone was faking profits. He heavily shorted the stock of Enron and its competitors, betting their price would drop, and very soon he looked like a mind reader. He is now managing one of the biggest and most famous hedge funds in America.

Dicey Characters

There are many admirable, exemplary personalities working in American finance today—people like Kovner, Peter Lynch, and John Bogle. There are also some awful narcissists, scammers, and fast-talkers. While researching this issue I read half a dozen autobiographies penned by Wall Street titans like George Soros, Victor Niederhoffer, James Cramer, and Michael Steinhardt. I can fairly say that this was some of the most painful literature I've crawled through in the last few years. Finance guys generally do not give piquant interviews either. Being an economic prodigy doesn't necessarily make you a fascinating person.

At times, some of the Wall Street lords come painfully close to embodying their enemies' caricatures of them as soulless, selfish, insecure, and venal. Steinhardt's book, for instance, provides extensive, at times sentimentalized, discussion of the shameless gambles, cheats, compulsions, cut corners, bald-faced lies, even crimes, of his father. This hardly inspires confidence in the more sophisticated financial manipulations of the son.

Ultimately, though, flaws in some of the masterminds don't make that much difference on Wall Street. Irresponsible or unethical actors can stir up great storms temporarily, and their periodic excesses feed the stereotypes of predatory financiers, undermining the credibility of straight-shooting compatriots who are far more numerous in our banks and brokerages. But the impressive thing about Wall Street is that, in the end, the system uses these dicey characters more than they use the system. Their manic talents get absorbed into the larger structure; their useful innovations become standard practices; in the process, the overall productivity of modern capitalism is ratcheted up. And their blemishes, if serious, eventually are exposed, leading to their personal downfall or marginalization. In time, the frauds and cheats will be unmasked on Wall Street—always. The stakes are too high, the results too immediate and too public, and the power too decentralized for any truly dishonest operator to last long before being outed by someone else. . . .

Keeping the Market Fair

So far, the public has been remarkably unpanicked. . . . To their credit, average Americans have not, as yet, let the dot-com bomb, the tech wreck, and the shenanigans of certain executives and Wall Street miscreants sour them on the value of private investing. But if the U.S. is to become a full-fledged investor nation, where every citizen is a yeoman capitalist with his own little piece of the national economic pie in the form of publicly traded stocks and bonds, then it is important we keep our markets and our corporations scrupulously clean and honest.

The good news is, that shouldn't be too hard. First, most American businesses already put heavy emphasis on upright behavior, if for no other reason than to keep their brand unsmirched. Second, our private markets have recently given . . . more or less the death penalty to Enron, Arthur Andersen, and several other companies that played fast and loose with their finances. This has reminded executives, bankers, and accountants what they risk when they cut corners. Third, the ferocious competition of free enterprise means there will be a race among firms to be part of the virtuous majority rather than the unethical minority. Already, [financial services company] Charles Schwab has launched an ad campaign touting its largely "self-serve" financial products as an alternative for investors upset with the conflicts of interest at some other brokerages.

To their credit, average Americans have not, as yet, let the dot-com bomb, the tech wreck, and the shenanigans of certain executives and Wall Street miscreants sour them on the value of private investing.

The biggest reason to be encouraged about our ability to keep investing square and fair is that U.S. capital markets are by far the most open, transparent, and honest in the world. We are much better off in this regard than Japan and the European continent, where stock markets have always been dominated by insiders and big boys. In Japan and Europe, the majority of all stock shares are held by banks and large companies, who often collude behind the scenes. In the U.S., the comparable figure is 7 percent.

A study of companies listed on stock exchanges in various countries found that in Germany, the five biggest shareholders in a typical corporation held 56 percent of its shares, on average. In France, the average was 58 percent. But in the U.S., the top five shareholders controlled just 25 percent, reports Brink

Lindsey [senior fellow at the CATO Institute]. Financial power is much more decentralized in America, which sharply reduces the likelihood of exploitative manipulation of holdings.

Sage Advice

The very best way for any individual to avoid stock market hypes and hustles is to follow the sage advice of [financial expert] Jim Glassman. . . . Forget buying the stock of the month, forget broker "tips," forget active trading altogether. Just buy a basket of equities that reflects a cross-section of U.S. business, sit back and hold those investments for the long run, and you will share in the broad progress of the American economy. It is a low-risk, almost foolproof way to make even modest-income families financially secure over a lifetime.

Mass investing can increase the quality of American life, reduce socio-economic disparities, and turn all citizens into full participants in our economy, rather than just wage serfs.

A decade or two ago, the strategy I've just described was easier said than done. But the wonderful democratization of investing that has taken place over the last generation has now made it possible to buy small increments of stocks and bonds cheaply, easily, and safely. Thanks to Vanguard, Ameritrade, Exchange Traded Funds, and many other such innovations, becoming a shareholder and wealth owner is now within the reach of even the smallest of the "little people." That is a great blessing, if we take advantage of it. Mass investing can increase the quality of American life, reduce socio-economic disparities, and turn all citizens into full participants in our economy, rather than just wage serfs.

5

The American Tax System Gives the Wealthy Too Much Power

Mark Zepezauer

Mark Zepezauer is a political cartoonist and author of The CIA's Greatest Hits; Boomerang! How Our Covert Wars Have Created Enemies Across the Middle East and Brought Terror to America; *and* Take the Rich Off Welfare.

While conservatives often complain about poor people on welfare, it is America's rich who benefit most from government giveaways. This welfare for the rich or "wealthfare" amounts to nearly a trillion dollars annually. With huge tax cuts, tax loopholes, and corporate subsidies, the rich are stealing from the poor and middle class at an unprecedented rate. As politicians subsidize America's wealthiest citizens with staggering wealth taken from honest taxpayers, the average American receives less and less in government services. Unless this trend is reversed, the U.S. Treasury will soon exist solely to empty the pockets of the middle class in order to hand the money over to the richest 1 percent of society.

Wealthfare—the money government gives away to corporations and wealthy individuals—costs us more than $815 billion a year. That's:

- 47 percent of what it costs to run the US government

(which is about $1.73 trillion a year, not counting en-
titlement trust funds like Social Security and Medicare)

- enough money to eliminate the federal debt in just over
eight years (the total is now $6.6 trillion, accumulated
over 200-plus years)

- more than four times what we spend on welfare for the
poor (currently around $193 billion a year). . . .

I've calculated these amounts as precisely as possible, but
they change every year, and data is often hard to obtain, so
they are, of course, estimates. If they seem high to you, cut
them all by 50 percent—or 75 percent; welfare for the rich
would still cost more than welfare for the poor.

In fact, $815 billion is definitely an underestimate. Limita-
tions of time and space forced me to leave out many major
categories of wealthfare. Most of these could be books in
themselves: state and local wealthfare (my figure includes just
federal giveaways), Medicare waste and fraud, automobile subsidies (much of which are state and local spending), the effects of Federal Reserve policies, the NAFTA [North American
Free Trade Agreement] and GATT [General Agreement on
Tariffs and Trade] treaties, foreign aid, deregulation of various
industries, fraudulent charitable deductions, the easy treatment given white-collar criminals, and on and on. . . .

Even within categories I do cite figures for, there are often
additional wealthfare expenses I haven't been able to nail
down. So there's no doubt that $815 billion greatly under-
states the amount of money American taxpayers lose each
year on welfare for the rich.

It's getting worse. . . .

Dreadful Corporate Welfare Programs

In 1996, the figure for total wealthfare was $448 billion a year.
By 1999, that number had grown to $603 billion. The 2003
estimate of $815 billion shows an 82 percent increase in just

seven years (or 69 percent if you adjust for inflation).

In contrast, spending for the poor rose only $63 billion (from the 1996 figure of $130 billion); taking inflation into account, that's a 41 percent increase. But in fact, spending that exclusively benefits the poor dropped by 10 percent in constant dollars. The only reason there was any increase at all is the vastly higher cost of Medicaid, which also serves some people who aren't poor.

In the intervening years, there's been a lot more discussion of wealthfare—and very little reform. In 1997, then-Representative John Kasich (R-OH) brought together a coalition of groups from both the right and the left to oppose a dozen especially dreadful corporate welfare programs. They managed to agree on the need to eliminate $11 billion—spread out over five years (in other words, about $2.2 billion a year, or less than half of one percent of what actually needed to be cut). Six years later, some of the programs they targeted have been cut back considerably, but every one of them still survives.

There's no doubt that $815 billion greatly understates the amount of money American taxpayers lose each year on welfare for the rich.

On the positive side, there have been small victories. Some especially odious nuclear boondoggles were canceled. The McNugget subsidy (an agricultural marketing program exploited by huge firms like McDonald's) was scaled back by 90 percent. Reformers have occasionally managed to keep things from getting worse. But overall, we've lost ground. . . .

[In 2004] both houses of Congress have passed a new generation of atrocious nuclear giveaways (though the two bills have yet to be reconciled and sent to the White House). The 2002 farm bill added another $73 billion in new subsidies. Despite then-bipartisan fervor for balancing budgets, the 1998 highway bill contained nearly 1,500 pork-barrel projects, cost-ing over $9 billion. Cutting the tax rate for long-term capital gains to 15 percent has more than doubled the amount of revenue lost to the US Treasury. The income cap on payroll taxes is now costing us 60 percent more than in 1996 (because the rich have gotten so much richer in the meantime).

Even when activists have worked for years to kill off inde-fensible programs, the funding has often shifted to less-scrutinized parts of the budget. According to Jim Riccio, who works on nuclear issues for Public Citizen [a public interest watchdog organization], "All those victories we've been getting have turned into lessons learned for industry and [federal] agencies, so they can make sure [such] victories never happen again."

It's not fair for people to get rich—and stay rich—by de-frauding people who are poorer than them.

Back when the Democrats controlled the Congress, their districts pulled in about $35 million more a year in goodies from Uncle Sam than GOP [the "Grand old Party" or Repub-lican Party] districts did. The Republicans complained might-ily about that, but then the Dem's districts did tend to have more poor people in them, who were presumably in need of federal assistance. But by 2001, after seven years of GOP con-trol, the well-heeled Republican districts were taking in, on average, $612 million more than those served by Democrats. That's a 1748 percent increase.

The Rich Are Stealing from the Poor

Before we go on, I'd like to clarify something. I'm not saying there's anything wrong with being rich, in and of itself. Many wealthy people earned their money by producing a product or a service the public liked and wanted to buy, or by helping a company do that. (The Grateful Dead are one example—their concerts became so popular that they had to run lotteries to decide who got to buy tickets.)

Speaking personally, I don't think that some people should inherit vast fortunes tax-free while others spend their whole lives scrambling to get by. And I believe that no one should live in luxury while others are starving. (That's not as hard to fix as you might think. A wealth tax of just 4 percent on the 200 richest people on earth would guarantee everyone enough to eat.)

Corporate welfare . . . tends to finance industries that pollute our air, water and soil, so we end up paying for them twice—with our money and with our health.

But this . . . isn't about those issues. . . . It's not fair for people to get rich—and stay rich—by defrauding people who are poorer than them. As you'll soon see, stealing from the poor—actually, from anybody who isn't rich—has become standard operating procedure in this country. In fact, the US government today functions mostly as a huge Robin-Hood-in-reverse.

But Doesn't It Help the Economy?

It is sometimes argued that corporate welfare benefits society as a whole by recirculating money back into the economy. Of course, that's even more true of welfare for the poor, which benefits grocery stores, supermarkets, clothing stores, land-lords, doctors, dentists, etc. Furthermore, many welfare programs pay for themselves many times over in future savings on health care, prisons, and welfare payments. (For example, according to conservative estimates, $1 invested in Head Start saves $3 in future costs to society.) Corporate welfare, on the other hand, tends to finance industries that pollute our air, water and soil, so we end up paying for them twice—with our money and with our health.

Subsidizing certain businesses or industries is not only unfair to competitors who aren't subsidized, but it also stifles the incentive of the subsidized businesses to innovate and develop new products (which might not be eligible for subsidies), ultimately making them less competitive.

Welfare for the rich fosters corruption, both in business and in government. And it's not uncommon for two wealthfare programs to conflict—as when the Interior Department subsidizes irrigation water for agribusinesses and the Agriculture Department pays those same companies not to grow crops with that water. (What do the companies do? Why, sell the water back to local governments at a profit, of course. What else?)

In any case, it's not as if the money currently spent on wealthfare would suddenly evaporate if we weren't handing it over to the rich. It would go into the economy some other way and would almost certainly have a more beneficial effect.

Wealthfare has one final cost: the creative talents of many bright lawyers, accountants, and financial advisors are spent figuring out how to squeeze the maximum benefit from our labyrinthine tax code. If they weren't wasting their time on that, they could be doing something genuinely useful, which would make the economy more productive for all of us.

Loopholes Are Worth More than Handouts

Welfare for the rich takes five basic forms. The first two are tax breaks and direct subsidies. The former are more insidious, for a couple of reasons. First, while subsidies typically have to be appropriated by Congress and signed into law by the president each year, tax breaks usually get little scrutiny, and since they don't have to be renewed annually, they last until they're repealed by some future tax law.

Second, while subsidies are usually for fixed amounts of money, the amount the government loses on a tax loophole depends on how many taxpayers take advantage of it each year, and to what extent. This means tax breaks are basically open-ended—there's no way the government can control, or even accurately predict, what they're going to cost. Furthermore, they're less controversial for politicians because everybody likes tax cuts; it's just that the tax cuts I talk about ... go only to certain groups.

To understand how money is spent in Washington, we have to make a distinction between budgets and bills. When the White House submits a budget to Congress every February, it's basically a suggestion. Then the Congressmembers pass their own budget, which is basically a set of spending guidelines for them to rely on (more or less loosely) as they pass their appropriations bills over the rest of the year. Theoretically, they've passed all those bills by October 1, reconciled between the House and Senate versions, and sent them to the president for signature.

If Congressmembers want to throw money at, say, nuclear power, they could budget for that every year and include it as an item in an appropriations bill. The other method is to write a tax break for nuclear power plant operators and get that passed and signed. Then it stands every year until it's repealed. Some tax breaks do come with a deadline, as with the "sunset" gimmicks in the [2004] tax bill that expire in 2006 or 2008 or 2010, unless some future Congress extends them. . . .

Over half of the $815 billion wealthfare figure comes from various tax breaks and loopholes. If you think that eliminating them amounts to raising taxes, that's fine; just be clear that you're saying the rich deserve to get more than $400 billion a year in tax breaks that aren't available to poorer people. . . . Tax breaks for the wealthy are government handouts, and they should be counted as that—welfare for the rich. Handouts are handouts. The only difference is that the rich don't need them.

Corporations Shift the Tax Burden to Individuals

Back in 1940, US corporations paid roughly half of the federal government's general revenues. Over the intervening years, business taxes have been steadily declining (except for a little blip in 1986). In fiscal year 1999, corporate tax payments dropped 2.5 percent and corporate profits rose 8.9 percent. Citizens for Tax Justice reported in 2002 that corporate tax payments were near record lows as a percentage of GDP (gross domestic product). Today, corporations pay just 7.4 percent. So if "fiscally responsible" candidates want to balance the budget and lower individual taxes, it's easy. All they have to do is tax corporations at the same rate as they did back when what was good for General Motors was good for the country.

The taxes corporations avoid paying have to be raised from individuals. Not all individuals, of course—that would be un-American. Thanks to a series of tax "reforms" that began in 1977, the rate paid by the richest Americans has been cut nearly in half, while Social Security taxes—which are paid overwhelmingly by ordinary wage earners, and not paid at all on income over $87,000—have steadily risen.

Now, I'm certainly no fan of the IRS, and I don't enjoy paying taxes any more than anybody else. (I'd probably enjoy it a bit more if I knew that more of it was going to fund worthwhile things like teachers and parks and hospitals.) But since corporations and wealthy individuals derive most of the benefit from what the government does, I think they should pay their fair share of taxes. They say they're in favor of free enterprise—let's pretend they mean it, and take them off the dole.

Fire Sales, Overruns, and Lazy Cops

The other three forms of welfare for the rich are more subtle than handouts or tax breaks. One is when Uncle Sam sells off properties belonging to We the People at a fraction of their true market value. You can find examples of this sort of boondoggle in . . . timber and mining subsidies. The magnificent trees in your national forests are being sold off to private interests for pennies on the dollar. But if you think that's bad, . . . on media subsidies and you'll find out [look at] . . . how much Uncle Sam charges radio and TV broadcasters for your public airwaves: nothing.

[The tax] rate paid by the richest Americans has been cut nearly in half, while Social Security taxes—which are paid overwhelmingly by ordinary wage earners . . . have steadily risen.

The flip side of the "fire sale" scam is when Uncle Sam shells out many times more than market value for goods and services from favored contractors. These cost overruns defraud the taxpayer, and seem to continue no matter who is elected (or appointed) to office. There are plenty of examples of this . . . [concerning] waste, fraud, and abuse in military spending. You've probably heard about the $640 toilet seat [paid by the Pentagon], but believe me, it gets much worse than that.

The fifth and final form of wealthfare might not sound like welfare at all, but it's a major aspect of how government policies favor the rich: the lax enforcement of white-collar crime. . . .

Miscellaneous Corporate Tax Breaks

Some economists make the following argument: Since corporations always pass their costs along to their customers, consumers ultimately pay all corporate taxes. Thus, there's really no such thing as corporate taxation. If this were true, then the lower the corporate tax rate, the higher consumer spending power would be. In the real world, however, the opposite is often the case.

In the 1950s, when the corporate tax rate was 52 percent and corporations paid almost a third of all income taxes, a single wage earner could support a family of four and could afford a new house, a car, and major appliances. In the 2000s, when the corporate tax rate ranges between 15 percent and 35 percent and corporations pay less than 10 percent of all income taxes, more than half of all families have two or more wage earners, and businesses are laying off people left and right. (According to the US Bureau of Labor Statistics, average earnings of nonsupervisory workers peaked in 1973, and they've been going down ever since. By 1992, they were 12 percent lower than they were in 1965.)

So it seems that corporations retain some of the savings they get from lower tax rates—which isn't surprising, since they lobby so ferociously for them. Their investment in certain key legislators can be repaid many times over.

For example, section 543(b) of the US tax code contains a provision that applies only to corporations formed in Nevada on January 27, 1972. It allows Cantor, Fitzgerald, and Co.— the only company incorporated in Nevada on that date—to exempt certain interest income involving securities and money-market funds from taxation.

Handcrafted tax breaks like this are nothing new. Movie mogul Louis B. Mayer had a provision inserted into the Revenue Act of 1951 that classified his retirement package as capital gains rather than ordinary income. As a result, it was taxed at 20 percent instead of 90 percent, and he saved nearly $2 million in federal taxes.

Fly the Friendly Skies

If there's any rationale for governmental subsidies, it would be to help useful fledgling technologies that might not otherwise be developed. The airline industry isn't exactly a newcomer anymore, and yet we taxpayers still fork out for the air traffic control system, hand out grants for airport construction, and provide reports from the National Weather Service. The industry receives $1 billion annually in federal military research funds, the taxpayer-funded Commerce Department lobbies aggressively for foreign purchases of US-built aircraft, and the airlines are exempted from the 4.3 cents per gallon fuel tax that the rest of us consumers pay.

But even with all these handouts (and there are plenty more . . .), commercial aviation has never been all that profitable. Even before the 9/11 attacks (which left the country's entire fleet grounded for a week or so), the industry was in a world of hurt. It was simply a case of over-capacity; compared to the demand, there were too many planes flying. Demand slacked off even more after 9/11, but the airlines ended up with a $15 billion bailout from Uncle Sugar that was triple what they had lost in the shutdown. And as with so many other wealthfare programs . . . , the lion's share of the bailout went to the biggest companies; many small firms received quite a bit less than they had lost in the 9/11 crisis.

So how did the big airlines show their gratitude? As you may recall, by laying off thousands of workers (who got absolutely no compensation from Congress) and shelling out huge bonuses for the executives. And did this elicit any outrage on Capitol Hill? Not particularly, though plenty of workers across the country were seething. In fact, Congress saw nothing wrong with setting up another $3 billion bailout for the airlines to get them through any economic turbulence arising from the war on Iraq. Welcome to the wonderful world of corporate welfare.

It's a system where the timber industry can spend $8 million lobbying to retain a threatened road-building subsidy and come up with $458 million in goodies. It's a world where [agricultural corporation] Archer Daniels Midland can spread around $3 million in campaign contributions and be rewarded with a $7 billion subsidy. It's a country where the tobacco companies can buy themselves a $50 billion tax break with a mere $30 million investment in "good government." And yes, it's your country; as the saying goes, these are your tax dollars at work.

6

The American Tax System Punishes the Wealthy

Bill Sizemore

Bill Sizemore is executive director of the Oregon Taxpayers Union, a statewide taxpayer organization that has helped place dozens of antitax measures on statewide ballots.

Whenever politicians propose tax cuts, liberals loudly complain that the benefits only go to the rich. However, the wealthy pay more into the tax system, which allows them to receive more money back when taxes are cut. This seems to matter little to those who want to take money from the rich so it can be redistributed to the less fortunate. This method of governance is called socialism and has been soundly rejected by Americans for decades. While the storybook character Robin Hood stole from the rich to give to the poor, the moral of that fairy tale has no place in modern society. Those with the talent, intelligence, or luck to become rich have no obligation to pay more than their fair share of taxes, despite the clamor of liberals and socialists.

After spending more than two decades publicly and privately debating liberals regarding the subject of taxation, one thing has become increasingly clear to me: Most liberals are socialists.

Liberals typically say that what bothers them most about our system of taxation is that the rich don't pay enough in

8

taxes, or that the wealthy don't shoulder their fair share of the tax burden. If you dig a little deeper, however, you will discover that is not what bothers them at all. It's something much worse.

Once you get past a liberal's, "it's just a tax cut for the rich" objection to every tax cutting measure ever proposed, some very interesting things become apparent. First, is this: To a liberal, tax policy should be fair to the poor, but absolutely must not be fair to the rich.

In fact, to liberals, wealthy Americans have absolutely no right to insist that the tax system treat them fairly. After all, they are rich and can look out for themselves. They can afford to pay more, therefore, they should.

This bias against successful people is evidenced by the consistency with which liberals attempt to stir up the pot of class envy at every turn. If a tax cutting bill or measure, for example, does nothing but give every taxpayer in every bracket, regardless of income, a 10 percent tax cut, to a liberal that tax cut is designed primarily to benefit the wealthy.

Why? Because mathematically the rich guy's 10 percent tax cut is bigger than the poor guy's 10 percent tax cut. The amount the rich guy saves is more than the amount the poor guy saves.

The Rich Pay More

It makes no difference to those on the political left, that when the dust settles, the rich guy still pays far more in taxes than the poor guy, or that the poor guy is a larger consumer of government services than the rich guy. None of that is even relevant to the typical liberal. Why? Because once again, that's not what really bothers them.

Here's what really bothers them: When the rich guy has paid all of his taxes and the check has cleared the bank, he still has more money left than the poor guy. That's it. That's what it's all about. No matter how much the rich guy pays in taxes, it will never be enough, because after he has paid, he still has more money than the poor guy.

It's not about how much the rich guy pays in taxes, or doesn't pay for that matter. It's about how much he has left over afterwards. It's about making sure that everyone has an equal share of the wealth, regardless of how much talent or creativity they possess or employ; and regardless of how much they actually produce.

The tax system is a tool for the promotion of socialism.

To the typical liberal, the tax system is merely a tool whereby government can redistribute the wealth in a manner he or she believes to be more equitable than the distribution that real life has meted; a tool for eliminating all of life's little inequities; or to the more radical among their ranks, the weapon by which they can strike a blow for all the little guys, who have been ripped off by the lords and masters of society.

Robbing from the Rich

The tax system is a tool for the promotion of socialism. Let me give you a real life example of how they think:

In 2000, I sponsored a ballot measure that would have made federal income taxes fully deductible on Oregon's state income tax returns. At the time the measure appeared on the ballot, Oregon had a legislatively imposed $3,000 cap on how much federal income tax a taxpayer could deduct on his state return. This meant, of course, that the "working poor" could deduct all of their federal taxes on their state tax returns, but those paying more than $3,000 in federal taxes were double taxed by the state of Oregon.

Simply stated, my proposal would have given to all taxpayers the same benefit the working poor already enjoyed. It would have ended the double taxation of income for every Oregon taxpayer regardless of his or her income bracket. What could be fairer? Nevertheless, you should have heard the hue and cry that went out across the land, when my measure was publicly announced. You would have thought I was proposing that we end taxes for the wealthy and make only poor people pay taxes.

As a society, we have a moral obligation to ensure that our tax system is fair to everyone, including the middle class and the more prosperous among us.

"Shameless tax cut for the wealthy. Sizemore would destroy the schools and put the poor and elderly out into the streets, just so he can give a tax out to his rich friends." That's the kind of rhetoric to which we were subjected day after day for several months.

During one of the many debates that were staged during the course of the campaign, I explained to one decidedly liberal audience, which had gathered in the sanctuary of one of the more liberal churches, that as a society, we have a moral obligation to ensure that our tax system is fair to everyone, including the middle class and the more prosperous among us. That statement seemed rather commonsensical and even moral to me.

My remarks, however, brought such looks of venom and utter disgust from the liberal audience, that I felt for a moment like the martyr Stephen before he was stoned. You could literally feel the anger and unrighteous indignation in the room. The very suggestion that taxes ought to be fair for those in the upper income brackets outraged them.

I am persuaded that the progressive income tax is something of a religious doctrine to the political left. They seem to believe that they have a moral right, even an obligation, to play Robin Hood; to rob the rich and give to the poor. Of course, they define *the rich* as anyone with a full time job.

[Novelist and promoter of capitalism] Ayn Rand was right about that, you know. Notwithstanding all the movies that make him a hero, the Robin Hood she described in her classic novel, *Atlas Shrugged,* was nothing more than a self-righteous thief. He took what didn't belong to him, and justified doing so simply because he thought someone else needed it more. Robbing from the rich to give to the poor has become official public policy in America.

Redistributing Wealth

It is quite possible that on the issue of tax fairness we conservatives have already lost the battle for the minds of the American people. Try this experiment on 10 everyday people, and you will see what I mean.

> *Robbing the rich by means of a progressive tax system and giving to the poor via welfare and other social programs has become the accepted way of life in America.*

Say to them, "Wouldn't you agree that our system of taxation in America is based upon the principle that we all pay taxes based upon our incomes, and that the money collected from the tax system is then spent by the government to provide programs that help the less fortunate among us. Is it not fair to describe the American system of taxation as one in which we all pay taxes to the government according to our ability, and then the government distributes the money out to our fellow Americans according to their individual needs?"

I have performed this little test several times. I usually conclude with one more question, stated something like this: A famous person once described such a tax system this way. He said, "from each according to his ability and to each according to his need." Do you agree with that statement? They usually say, "Yes." Do you know who made it? They usually say, "No.

Very few Americans seem to be aware that the author of that statement was the communist philosopher, Karl Marx, or that a highly progressive income tax system is a foundational stone of communist doctrine.

Robbing the rich by means of a progressive tax system and giving to the poor via welfare and other social programs has become the accepted way of life in America. Why should a tax system have to be fair to the poor when it is okay to rob them outright, as long as it is for a good cause?

Telling a liberal that the top one percent of the taxpayers in America pay 30 percent of total taxes is a total waste of breath. They don't care. The fact is irrelevant. If, after they have paid their taxes, the rich still have more money than the poor, they obviously aren't paying enough.

Yes, most liberals are socialists. No question about it. Their goal is to redistribute the wealth by means of government coercion. To me that fact is settled. Our real dilemma is this: Much of the American public has bought their doctrine and are just as much socialists at heart as they are.

This has always been a very slippery slope, you know. Once a society allows its government to levy taxes to finance even one worthwhile, charitable cause, the floodgates begin to open. From that point on, the question of socialism is merely a matter of degree.

7

Rich Celebrities Have Too Much Political Influence

Darrell M. West

Darrell M. West is the author of thirteen books, including Air Wars: Television Advertising and Election Campaigns, 1952–2004; Celebrity Politics, the Rise and Fall of the Media Establishment; *and* Patrick Kennedy: The Rise to Power. *West is also professor of public policy and political science at Brown University.*

Americans love celebrities, and popular music, television, sports, and movie stars have become increasingly influential in politics. Whether they are Republicans or Democrats, wealthy rock stars, comedians, and movie idols can draw large crowds to political fund-raisers. In a country where a candidate for the Senate or state government needs to raise tens of millions of dollars to run for office, celebrities help to attract widespread media attention along with money and votes. With photogenic faces and the ability to speak as political outsiders, celebrities hold a distinct advantage over experienced policy makers in America's star-struck culture. A political system based on superficial celebrity worship is not good for the nation. Unless Americans start to value policy experts and experienced lawmakers over music and movie stars, participatory democracy will fall victim to ignorance, apathy, and media manipulation.

Darrell M. West, "American Politics in the Age of Celebrity," *The Hedgehog Review,* Spring 2005, pp. 59–65. Copyright © 2005 by the Institute for Advanced Studies in Culture. Reproduced by permission.

It is the Age of Celebrity in the United States. Movie stars run for elective office and win. Politicians play fictional characters on television shows. Rock stars raise money for political parties. Musicians, athletes, and artists speak out on issues of hunger, stem cell research, and foreign policy. While this is not the first time celebrities have sought elective office or spoken out on questions of public policy, there are a number of factors in the contemporary period that have accentuated celebrity politics and given it a far greater prominence. The culture has changed in ways that glorify fame and fortune. The news industry has become highly competitive. Media reporters need good copy, and few sources provide better copy than actors, athletes, and entertainers. The fact that politics has become very expensive places a premium on those who can convince others to give money.

In this essay, I describe what factors have contributed to the blurring of the lines between politics and entertainment, how politicians mimic celebrities (and vice versa), what the age of celebrity reveals about our culture, and what risks a celebrity culture faces. In important respects, the contemporary period has undergone crucial changes, sometimes to the detriment of society as a whole. In particular, at a time when the press pays closer attention to celebrities speaking out on complex policy subjects than to experts with detailed knowledge, there is a danger that politics will be drained of substance, and serious deliberation and discourse will be diminished. If politics becomes an entertainment show based on performance skills, society loses its capacity for nuance, compromise, and deliberation.

Blurring the Lines Between Politics and Entertainment

Celebrity politics is not a new phenomenon. In the eighteenth and nineteenth centuries, it was common in the United States for famous families and former military generals to use their prominence as an asset to gain elective office. Many of our leading presidents were famous for their exploits on the military field, including George Washington, Andrew Jackson, William Henry Harrison, and Ulysses S. Grant, whose military fame led them to high office. Other historical leaders were legacy politicians who came from celebrated families such as the Roosevelts, Adams, and Harrisons. These three families produced six presidents (Theodore and Franklin Roosevelt, John and John Quincy Adams, and William Henry and Benjamin Harrison). When Blair Lee was elected governor of Maryland in the 1970s, he was the 21st member of his extended family to hold political office since 1647. According to Stephen Hess, 700 families account for "1,700 of the 10,000 men and women who have been elected to the federal legislature since 1774."

The press pays closer attention to celebrities speaking out on complex policy subjects than to experts with detailed knowledge.

Throughout American history, celebrated writers and non-politicos have spoken out on issues of the day. Mark Twain's political satire and quips twitted many a prominent public figure. Ernest Hemingway was involved in a number of foreign and domestic controversies of his era. Charles Lindbergh gained fame as the first pilot to fly solo, nonstop across the Atlantic. He then used this prominence to lead America's isolationist movement in the 1930s and 1940s.

Several trends over the past few decades, however, have contributed to a celebrity culture that is far more pronounced and politically important than in earlier epochs.

Fundamental shifts in media have blurred the lines between politics and entertainment. With the rise of new technologies such as cable television, talk radio, and the Internet, the news business has become very competitive and more likely to focus on gossip and prominent personalities. Tabloid shows such as *Access Hollywood,* which attract millions of viewers, glorify celebrities and provide a "behind-the-scenes" look at the entertainment industry, with reporters staking out "star" parties and nightclubs and reporting on who is in attendance. The old "establishment" press that kept rumors of President John F. Kennedy's marital infidelities out of the newspapers has been replaced by a news media that specializes in reporting on the private lives of politicians and Hollywood stars. Individuals who have drinking problems or drug habits, or gamble too much, are likely to find themselves in today's news. Reporters are now more likely to focus on human features than detailed substance. According to William Winter, who was one of America's first television news broadcasters in 1950, the modern era is a time when news broadcasts are "increasingly shallow and trivial." Competition in American politics centers around who can reduce complex messages down to understandable, nine-second (or, more recently, five-second) sound bytes.

In order to guarantee a large turnout at a fundraising party, it has become common to feature comedians, singers, and other celebrities who can attract a large crowd.

The growing cost of American campaigns has also contributed to the emergence of celebrity politics. Needing money to finance television ads and get-out-the-vote drives, politicians have become fundraising machines. Senators in large states must raise $5,000 a day every day of their six-year term in order to have enough money for their re-election efforts. Without large amounts of money, candidates cannot run television ads or mobilize likely voters. This need for cash forces politicians into alliances with athletes, actors, and artists who can headline fundraising events. In order to guarantee a large turnout at a fundraising party, it has become common to feature comedians, singers, and other celebrities who can attract a large crowd. In the 2004 presidential election, Bruce Spring-steen gave a series of concerts to raise money to defeat President George W. Bush, and other Hollywood celebrities such as actors Sean Penn, Mike Farrell, and Linda Ronstadt spoke out against the Iraq War. With their strong support in "red" states, Republicans relied on country singers, and individuals such as Garth Brooks lent their names to the cause of electing Republicans across the country.

The intertwining of politics and entertainment has blurred the lines between these two fields. The old days when entertainers and politicians led more or less separate existences has been replaced with a system that regularly brings members of each club into close contact with the other side.

How Politicians Mimic Celebrities (and Vice Versa)

In today's world, politicians need celebrities and celebrities need politicians—each possesses attributes that the other requires. From the standpoint of politicians, celebrities are a way to reach voters jaded by political cynicism. In the 1950s, two-thirds of Americans trusted the government in Washington to do what is right. Presidents had high moral authority, and citizens had confidence in the ethics and morality of their leaders. However, following scandals in Vietnam and Watergate, economic stagflation, and controversies over Iran-Contra and Monica Lewinsky, the public became far less trusting. They are no longer confident about political leaders and are less likely to trust their motives. When asked whether they trust the government in Washington to do what is right, two-thirds express mistrust. Citizens feel that politicians are in it for themselves and that they serve special interests. A citizenry that trusts its politicians to tell it the truth has been replaced by a public that is highly skeptical about motives and intentions. In this situation, it is difficult for politicians to raise money and build public support; they simply do not have the credibility necessary, for political persuasion. They need to associate themselves with people who have higher credibility than they themselves do—people, in other words, from outside the political realm who are considered more trustworthy and less partisan, and who have high credibility with the general public.

Celebrities are seen as white knights, not tainted by past partisan scandals or political dealings, who can clean up the political establishment and bring new ideas to public policymaking.

Politicians love to draw on athletes, musicians, and actors because they come from outside the political world. In many cases, celebrities are seen as white knights, not tainted by past partisan scandals or political dealings, who can clean up the political establishment and bring new ideas to public policymaking. Plus, they are seen as too rich to be bought. Their fame attracts press coverage and campaign contributors. Journalists crowd their press conferences and strain to hear everything they say about issues of foreign and domestic policy. Even though they lack detailed knowledge on these issues, they have a platform that allows them to participate in civic discourse.

These were central assets in Arnold Schwarzenegger's campaign for governor of California [in 2003] and his election demonstrates why celebrities are effective in running for office and speaking out on public affairs. Seeking office at a time when three-quarters of state voters thought California was headed in the wrong direction and when the incumbent governor, Gray Davis, had a job approval rating hovering around twenty percent, the Hollywood actor campaigned for change and reform, and said that, having spent most of his life outside the political world, he was better equipped than career politicians to bring about necessary changes.

Politicians form alliances with celebrities and use them to raise money, attract media attention, and persuade recalcitrant voters, but celebrities also need politicians. In today's rapidly changing world, celebrities feel pressure to keep their names in the news, and it is a long time between movies or concert tours. Having a charitable or political cause is one way to keep one's name before the public and gets one a spot on talk and entertainment shows. While celebrities generally prefer non-controversial causes such as more money for children living in poverty or breast cancer research, increasingly entertainment figures are taking stances on controversial subjects, such as the Iraq War and election campaigns.

There used to be concern about celebrities' images getting tangled up in political controversies. Dating back to [actress] Jane Fonda's opposition to the Vietnam War and the resulting political backlash among veterans upset with her visit to Hanoi [in 1972], celebrities have worried that too much political involvement could damage their careers. However, in recent years, the large number of entertainers taking active political positions suggests that there is far less concern about negative fallout than would have been the case a few decades ago. There is safety in numbers: as long as many celebrities are politically active, there is far less danger that any one of them will suffer a debilitating backlash from his or her political activities. The activism of some encourages activism by other celebrities.

What the Age of Celebrity Says About Us

The Age of Celebrity is a cultural lens that reveals what Americans value, for it is clear that celebrityhood is as much about us as it is about prominent people. Celebrity culture is not something that is being inflicted on an unwilling public. Rather, it is a development that people watch and willingly participate in. Tabloid newspapers have a large circulation: *The National Enquirer* sells around 2.3 million copies every week, and *Star* magazine has a circulation of l.7 million. Television shows devoted to gossip about the famous do well. An average of 3.5 million viewers watch the syndicated television show *Inside Edition,* and the E! Entertainment network attracts several million viewers to its shows about Hollywood figures. Celebrities dominate the list of personalities that people would like to meet. A national survey of teenagers found they would most like to meet musicians, followed by athletes and actors—politicians were well down the list.

A national survey of teenagers found they would most like to meet musicians, followed by athletes and actors— politicians were well down the list.

Not only are people fascinated with famous individuals and their personal lives, they want to be on television themselves. Indeed, their quest for fame is so strong they are willing to eat rats or betray loved ones to achieve stardom. Note the popularity of "reality-based" television shows. The final episode of the first season of *Survivor* earned ratings that were second only to the Super Bowl. The popularity of this genre led pollsters to ask a national sample what they would be willing to allow a reality show to film them doing. The most popular results were 31 percent for being in their pajamas, 29 percent for kissing, 26 percent for crying, 25 percent for having an argument with someone, 16 percent for being drunk, 10 percent for eating a rat or insect, 8 percent for being naked, and 5 percent for having sex. This "democratization" of fame, first described by [actor and author] Leo Braudy many years ago, allows people of ordinary means and talent to become "temporary" celebrities.

Based on these trends, it is clear that the cult of personality, resonates with many Americans and is alive and well in society at large. Viewers love to hear tidbits about celebrity lives, even what these individuals think about political issues of the day, America is a voyeuristic society that values news and information about prominent people as well as ordinary people who have fleeting moments of fame.

The Risks of Celebrity Politics

America's celebrity politics makes for an entertaining show. It is interesting to see a former wrestler such as Jesse Ventura win the governorship of a major state [Minnesota] or Schwarzenegger win the California gubernatorial election. Hillary Clinton's [in 2000] campaign for Senate attracted considerable interest, as did the campaigns of various "third-generation" Kennedys from around the country. But there is more at stake than merely entertainment in the rise of celebrity culture, particularly in the political arena.

At one level, this celebrity regime might be beneficial to our culture and to our political system. Celebrities could bring new ideas to the process. Unlike conventional politicians, celebrities do not have to serve a long apprenticeship before they run for major offices. In a world where entangling alliances are the rule, these individuals are as close to free agents as one can find. This freedom might allow them to challenge the conventional wisdom, adopt unpopular stances, and expand the range of ideas represented in our national dialogue. Since they are not conventional politicians and are not limited to mainstream coalitions based on Left or Right, they have a greater potential to innovate than career politicians.

But in other respects, a system based on celebrityhood raises a host of problems. Our fascination with celebrities raises the risk that there will be more superficiality and less substance in our political process. Celebrities have contributed to the circus atmosphere that has arisen in American politics; increasingly, politics has become a matter of public performance. Politicians get judged more by their ability to deliver crisp sound bytes than by their substantive knowledge. With journalists interested in celebrity quotes and good copy, experts with detailed knowledge about public policy are more likely to become marginalized. It is easier to go to the famous and get their opinion than to seek out voices of less prominent people who may actually know more.

National surveys document that more than ten percent of Americans get information about politics from late-night entertainment shows such as *The Tonight Show* or *Letterman*. And for those under the age of thirty years old, that figure rises to nearly half. As the network news has emphasized entertainment features and lifestyle stories at the expense of hard news, more and more Americans are turning to entertainment shows such as *The Daily Show with Jon Stewart* for political commentary.

Conventional politicians are being replaced by famous, media-savvy fundraisers.

Both democracy and culture depend on deliberation, participation, and engagement. But what we have now is a system where star power is weighted more heavily than traditional political skills, such as bargaining, compromise, and experience. Conventional politicians are being replaced by famous, media-savvy fundraisers. The quality of civic deliberation is becoming trivialized. The gossip quotient has increased, and politics has become a 24-hour entertainment spectacle. With attention spans for important stories dropping precipitously, the system rewards celebrity politicians with famous names. Unless these individuals provide citizens with proper information, it short-circuits our system of governance. Without quality information, voters cannot make informed choices about their futures.

American politics has never placed a strong emphasis on substance. Compared to other Western democracies, fewer people vote at election time, and many appear not to be very informed about their decisions. As celebrity politics takes root, there is the long-term danger that citizens will become even less knowledgeable about policy choices, and they may become content to watch and be entertained. But elections are a key device by which representative democracy takes place. Citizens must feel engaged in the process, must be able to think about their options, and must feel they have a stake in the important decisions that get made. Without serious deliberation and discourse, politics becomes mere entertainment. Without experience and knowledge, society may lose its ability to confront pressing problems and resolve social conflict.

8

Celebrities Have Little Influence on Voters

Kevin Baron

Kevin Baron is a writer and researcher living in Washington, D.C.

Every four years, during U.S. presidential campaigns, the world's most famous faces are seen at political conventions. In 2004 the Democratic convention in Boston drew some of the most well-known liberal stars in Hollywood, including actors Ben Affleck and Alec Baldwin. Critics on both sides of the political aisle grumbled about celebrity influence on voters. However, studies show that people are not swayed by celebrity endorsements. Voters do not support candidates simply because they are backed by movie stars or famous musicians. As much as Americans love celebrities, there is little evidence that powerful stars can sway the electorate.

[D]emocratic] convention week headliners [in August 2004] drew gavel-to-gavel coverage and scrutiny as reporters picked apart the issue messages, personal backgrounds, and political motivation of . . . Ben Affleck and Alec Baldwin.

Celebrity politicking has been part of the American political landscape at least since President Grover Cleveland shook hands at the White House with bare-knuckle champion John L. Sullivan, who despite being a wife-beating, womanizing, racist drunk, was more known and admired than the presi-

Kevin Baron, "Do Celebrities Make a Difference?" *The Boston Globe,* August 1, 2004. Copyright © 2004 by The New York Times Company. Reproduced by permission of the author.

ident in his time: [In 2004] Boston did its best to rival the flood of personalities at the 2000 Democratic convention in Hollywood's own backyard, reeling in everyone from party stalwarts like Rob Reiner and the Baldwin brothers to all-purpose Hollywood B-list partygoers to the ubiquitous Affleck, who gave [TV show host] Katie Couric a tour of Boston (Fenway Park, his mother's house, a cheeseburger joint) on "Good Morning America." . . .

Everyone wants boldface names at their parties and panel discussions. But just what are celebrities good for in politics?

Some came to Boston last week to lend their support to [presidential candidate John] Kerry, while others came to advance a particular cause. [U2 singer] Bono, for example, came to talk to policy makers and future officeholders about the global AIDS crisis and Third World debt, and will be taking his show to the Republican convention next month [in September 2004] as well. Rap music mogul Russell Simmons promoted the voter registration drive sponsored by his Hip Hop Summit Action Network, and insisted to CNN that the group's celebrity panel discussion on political issues drew full houses.

Others were here to party and grease the wheels of fundraising. But while Hollywood is to Democrats what the oil industry is to Republicans (with donations evenly matched dollar for dollar, according to the Center for Responsive Politics), most of the stars roaming the convention floor and prowling the parties are not themselves major movie-business donors. Instead, they play the role of carnival barkers and hostesses, drawing into the Big Top those civilian spenders capable of donating or raising tens of millions of dollars.

The Message Doesn't Ring True

Nor are celebrities really expected to swing many votes. According to Michael X. Delli Carpini, dean of the Annenberg School for Communications at the University of Pennsylvania, the few studies he has seen that attempt to measure celebrity influence on voters show that direct appeals, such as automated celebrity phone messages to random voters, are ineffective. "They don't work," said Delli Carpini. "They don't have the ability to motivate people to get involved." It's not clear whether it's the celebrity, the canned phone call, or the combination of "the celebrity and the message that doesn't ring true."

"I don't think people vote one way or another because a star has endorsed a candidate or not," said Marty Kaplan, director of The Norman Lear Center and associate dean of the Annenberg School for Communication at the University of Southern California [USC], and a former deputy campaign manager for Walter Mondale's 1984 presidential bid. Besides, adds Kathleen Hall Jamieson, director of the Annenberg Public Policy Center at the University of Pennsylvania, the association with the candidate is much more likely to influence perception of the celebrity than the other way around.

"I don't think people vote one way or another because a star has endorsed a candidate or not."

The Creative Coalition, which bills itself as "the premier nonprofit, nonpartisan social and political advocacy organization of the entertainment industry," made headlines with its $1,000-a-plate gala at Louis Boston [restaurant] on Wednesday featuring a performance by the Red Hot Chili Peppers, a host committee of 32 members of Congress, and perhaps the week's biggest haul of celebrities.

But Robin Bronk, the group's executive director, said the Creative Coalition wasn't about glitz but about issues: First Amendment rights, arts education, the offshoring of film and television production jobs. (The Boston gala was cosponsored by the Recording Industry Association of America, which leads the fight against Internet music piracy.) "Our spokespeople for issues are vested in that issue," said Bronk. "The issue means something personally to them . . . just like any activist."

By all accounts, most of today's politically active celebrities support Democrats. (The Creative Coalition also plans to hold similar events at the Republican convention in New York next month, though so far only 10 members of Congress and a handful of celebrities outside the organization's leadership have signed on to the New York gala, according to their website.)

A Conservative Backlash

As a result, most criticism of celebrity involvement in politics comes from conservative media. A review of news transcripts during the run-up to the Iraq war shows that the amount of coverage defending a celebrity's right to voice a protest pales in comparison to the volumes of anticelebrity criticism from the right, whether it was the *New York Post's* blast at "Baghdad Sean" Penn or the beating the Dixie Chicks [county singers] took for daring to criticize George W. Bush directly.

"In the Iraq war there was a lot of sound and fury on the right condemning stars for speaking up, usually on the basis of 'How dare they, what right do they have, what do they know,'" said USC's Kaplan.

In fact, conservative pundits shouted against "Hollywood elites" and "star-dumb" so loudly and frequent that soon mainstream news outlets were running stories reporting an alleged public "backlash" against celebrities. Their case was based on such flimsy evidence as Internet chat room chatter and junk polls on the AOL.com and MTV homepages asking if celebrities should speak up or shut up. Also cited was an Internet petition drive called Citizens Against Celebrity Pundits, launched by a homemaker from North Carolina, which reportedly gathered more than 100,000 signatures.

Most media scholars interviewed dismiss claims that there is a pervasive anticelebrity movement among Americans. In the end, says USC's Kaplan, it all comes down to partisan politics. "If you are a Republican, it's just wonderful if [California governor] Arnold Schwarzenegger has strong views about politics, but it's not wonderful if Alec Baldwin does."

9

Corporations Use Their Power to Benefit the Rich

Multinational Monitor

Multinational Monitor is a monthly magazine devoted to examining the activities of multinational companies.

Since the 1970s decisions made by self-interested politicians and corporate officers have caused great harm to America's lower and middle classes. By using their power to enact billions in tax cuts for the rich, squelch union organization, and oppose minimum wage increases, corporations have helped the wealthy become wealthier. Meanwhile, the rest of the population struggles with unemployment, astronomical consumer debt, and the greatest income disparities since the 1920s. Unless something is done to address the widening chasm between rich and poor, the United States will become less democratic and fewer opportunities will be available for the majority of American citizens.

The last 30 years has seen a tremendous rise in income and wealth disparity in the United States, and around the world. . . .

The share of national wealth owned by the richest 1 percent has doubled during the past three decades. . . . Income inequality has skyrocketed nearly as fast.

These are startling changes in the relative affluence of the country's population over a very short period. They leave the country more class bound, less democratic, less just and more riven by wealth and inequality gaps that mean people's basic life opportunities are unequal.

Most of the increased wealth created over the last three decades has been captured by a small sliver of the population.

While the well off have become better off and the rich have become opulently so, the middle and lower groups have struggled to stay in place. It took until the late 1990s for the inflation-adjusted average wage of the bottom 80 percent of the population to catch up with the levels of the early 1970s. Wealth of the richest 1 percent has skyrocketed, while personal and consumer debt has ballooned for those in the middle and bottom.

Shifting Power Relationships

There was nothing inevitable about these trends, and no forces of nature prevent them from being reversed. Rather, the rise in wealth and income inequality is due to shifting power relationships and policy choices favoring the rich, each of which reinforce each other. Capital has grabbed power from labor, and corporations have taken power from citizens. The federal government, as well as state and local governments, have pursued policies—from trade to labor law—that have strengthened corporate power and weakened workers.

Capital has grabbed power from labor, and corporations have taken power from citizens.

A vicious cycle has ensued, with corporations then better positioned to lobby and advocate for still more policy changes to shift income, wealth and power.

There are too many intertwined factors driving the growth in inequality to identify them all, or to separate out the relative contribution of each, but it is important to pinpoint specific contributing causes. Identifying these factors is a prerequisite to remedying or addressing each, and ultimately to reversing the trends of rising inequality. Focusing on the policies and trends driving inequality is important in order to dispense with the myth that growing inequality is inevitable (to this, it should be enough to cite [scholar] Edward Wolff's point that wealth inequality in the United States actually fell steadily from the period of the Great Depression until the early or mid-1970s), or simply the outgrowth of new technologies. Detailing the causes of inequality is also important because it makes clear the many ways in which the recent era of enhanced corporate rule and corporate globalization has not led to broadly shared benefits, but to modest gains in wealth that have been appropriated by a relative few.

With that in mind, here are [some] of the more important contributing factors to surging inequality in the United States.

Falling Levels of Unionization

Unions now represent less than 10 percent of the workforce in the private sector in the United States. Yet they still represent the single best means for workers to improve their economic conditions. There is a more than 28 percent wage premium for union membership in the United States—meaning the single fact of belonging to a union raises the average worker's wage more than 28 percent—and it is far higher in the area of benefits.

But even reference to the dramatic wage premium understates the importance of unions. Union power is collective power. When unions represent a higher proportion of the workforce—when there is greater "union density"—in a particular industry, unions can raise the overall industry wage rate, including for non-union workers. When unions represent a higher proportion of the national workforce, they can raise the national wage rate.

Even more importantly, when there is greater national union density, unions can exert more political power, to ensure the benefits and pain in the national economy is more equally shared. . . .

The erosion of the U.S. manufacturing base, vicious anti-union campaigns by employers and inadequate organizing efforts by labor has led to the drop-off in union representation in the United States.

Corporate Globalization

The corporate globalization trade regime—manifested in the rules of the World Trade Organization and other trade agreements—has freed corporations to locate production anywhere in the world for sale anywhere in the world. . . . Millions of high-paying manufacturing jobs have been lost in the United States as a result.

Workers who remain in the manufacturing sector are forced to compete in the race to the bottom, with union demands for wage gains replaced by employer demands for wage givebacks. Sometimes the employers really are unable to compete with lower-wage producers in other countries (sometimes they are those lower-wage producers). Sometimes the employers simply use the threat to enhance profitability. Either way, workers bargaining leverage is dramatically lessened. Workers lose. Owners win.

Corporate globalization diminishes the union base and worker power.

Moreover, the exact same threats are among the most effective at deterring workers from joining unions. Join a union, employers tell workers in the majority of organizing campaigns, and we'll have to close. We just can't compete if we are burdened by union wages and union bureacracy (read: protection for worker rights).

Nowhere is the intertwined nature of the causes of inequality made more clear. Corporate globalization diminishes the union base and worker power. Weaker unions are less able to defend their jobs, either in direct negotiations with companies or in policy-making disputes in Congress. And on and on.

Declining Minimum Wage

One way to place a floor on the downward push on wages is to maintain a respectable minimum wage. Because the minimum wage in the United States is set periodically, and not pegged to inflation, it is forever losing value, though periodically bumped up a bit when the drop gets severe and the political moment makes it hard for Republicans to defeat a minimum wage rise. There has been no progress whatsoever in the obvious solution to this problem, which is to raise the minimum wage and then peg it to the inflation rate, so that it rises along with the cost of living. Low-wage industries—led by the restaurant association—have led the Chamber of Commerce and the major national business lobbies to oppose minimum wage hikes.

Today's minimum wage of $5.15 has been stuck since 1997. In inflation-adjusted terms, its current value is almost a quarter less than at its peak in the late 1960s.

In one of the most vibrant economic justice campaigns in the United States today, many communities have passed living wage laws, requiring employers to pay not just a minimum wage, but a minimum wage sufficient to enable a family to survive. Unfortunately, these laws typically apply only to government contractors, or sometimes to recipients of government benefits, but not to the overall community. They are an important step forward, and provide some hope for the future; but for now have not managed to have broad nationally felt impacts on wage rates.

The Soaring Stock Market

Although the market has come back down to earth to more reasonable levels in the last couple years, it has grown drammatically over the last three decades. The "sustainable" part of this stock market rise—meaning stock prices justifiable in relationship to earnings, or profits, and the prospect for future profits—reflects spikes of very high profits, including in the mid-1990s. Those high profits themselves were due to a variety of factors, but among them were the increased reliance on overseas manufacturing and monopolistic markets enabling corporations to impose excessive prices on consumers.

Popular myth to the contrary, the stock market gains accrued overwhelmingly to the rich. . . . Stock holdings are as concentrated now as they have been historically.

Tax Cuts for the Rich

Although the federal tax code remains somewhat progressive—meaning higher income earners pay a higher proportion of their income in taxes than lower earners—it is less so than it has been historically. The Reagan and [George W.] Bush tax cuts have massively reduced the tax take from the rich, and the . . . proposed Bush tax cut [in 2005] would reduce the level still further. More than a third of the value of the current Bush proposal would accrue to the richest 1 percent of taxpayers, according to Robert McIntyre of Citizens for Tax Justice. Nearly half of the benefit would go to the richest 5 percent of taxpayers.

State taxes, heavily reliant on sales tax, remain regressive; and the current state funding deficit is likely to lead states to increase regressive taxes. . . .

Thanks to tax code revisions and fancy tax sheltering, the corporate share of paid federal taxes is down to approximately 7 percent—compared to 22 percent level in the 1960s.

Deprivations of the Poor

The last three decades have seen a steady decline in traditional welfare payments to the poor, leaving them considerably worse off. . . . At the same time as they have cut welfare for the poor, local, state and federal governments have become far more generous in making gifts to the corporate welfare kings. To take two indicators: in just the period from the 1970s to the 1990s, corporate bailouts have grown from the level of hundreds of millions of dollars to hundreds of billions of dollars. The defense budget, which serves corporate welfare as much as any other purpose, has soared under the Reagan and Bush II administrations—a simple transfer from taxpayers to Lockheed, Boeing, Raytheon and their shareholders.

At the same time as they have cut welfare for the poor, local, state and federal governments have become far more generous in making gifts to the corporate welfare kings.

The banking system systematically deprives lower-income and minority communities of the credit they need to build up investments and wealth. The services that are provided come increasingly from shady and price-gouging check-cashing operations and payday lenders. Meanwhile, the super-aggressive marketing of credit cards to middle-income people has led many to fall deep into debt, and forced to pay off huge accumulated debts at usurious interest rates.

Although it has loosened its grip on the money supply in recent years, at crucial periods over the last three decades the Fed has driven up interest rates and plunged the economy in recession. The resultant high unemployment rates diminished worker power and pushed down wages.

A Culture of Overcompensation

Although the routinization of obscenely high executive pay directly affects too few people to meaningfully impact overall income inequality, it has created a culture in which professionals and people in upper-income groups expect to be paid very generously. New class-based social norms have emerged about what constitutes a reasonable salary, and how much a person "needs" to get by—what upper-income groups view as necessity is of course unavailable to most people in the country.

This culture, nurtured by new marketing campaigns advertising luxurious lifestyles and a media that more and more narrowly targets upper-income groups, has helped push up salaries broadly at the top.

But these riches are not available to all. Part of the culture has been the normalization and acceptance of a persistent and deepening income and wealth inequality, with the situation of middle and lower income groups largely absent from the news or popular culture.

10

Corporations Use Their Power to Benefit All Sectors of Society

Radley Balko

Radley Balko is a policy analyst for the Cato Institute, a libertarian public policy institute in Washington, D.C.

Activists and politicians often vilify America's corporate officers as being coldhearted and mercenary. These critics rarely mention, however, the great benefits provided to society by powerful CEOs who run profitable and efficient corporations. Such companies provide jobs, security, and indispensable products that benefit everyone. Meanwhile, corporations run for altruistic purposes have often failed, leaving workers and stockholders with nothing. America's wealth and competitiveness depend on profit-minded CEOs with the power to shape American economic policies.

In the United States, the . . . professional and political world buzzes with phrases like "corporate governance," "corporate citizenship," and "social responsibility." The same, I am sad to hear, is becoming true of Hong Kong. Corporations today are regularly scolded by consumer activists and politicians who implore them to eschew profit-seeking every now and then for more conscientious endeavors. The implication is that there is something cold and inhumane about the raw and rugged free market—that the profit motive alone isn't sufficiently altruistic to turn loose on polite society.

Nothing could be further from the truth. The mid-20th century American writer Isabel Paterson put it best in her book *The God of the Machine* when she wrote, "Most of the harm in the world is done by good people, and not by accident, lapse, or omission . . . innumerable speculative thinkers, inventors, and organizers, have contributed to the comfort, health, and happiness of their fellow men—because that was not their intention."

A Tale of Two Companies

In the 1990s, a corporate executive named Aaron Feuerstein quickly became the darling of the American media. Feuerstein oversaw a Massachusetts-based textiles company called Malden Mills. In 1995, three of Malden Mills' factories burned to the ground. Feuerstein was pronounced a corporate hero when he promised his workers that he would continue to pay their salaries out of his own pocket while he rebuilt the factories, even though his workers wouldn't be producing.

For every job [General Electric CEO Jack Welsh] slashed, he eventually created dozens of new ones.

As a result, Feuerstein was invited to speak at colleges and universities all across the U.S. He was given honorary degrees, and was the subject of a flattering profile on the television program *60 Minutes.*

Contrast Feuerstein with former General Electric CEO Jack Welch. During his tenure, Welch was considered by many to be the epitome of the ruthless, coldhearted, profit-minded corporate executive. He laid off thousands of workers in his efforts to streamline and change the focus of the company. Wall Street loved him. Newspaper editorial boards and activists hated him. To make matters worse, as Welch was preparing to step down from General Electric a few years ago, a divorce trial revealed him to be the recipient of extravagant benefits paid for by GE stockholders.

But here's where the tale gets interesting. Feuerstein's pledge to continue paying his workers eventually cost them their jobs, and cost Feuerstein his company. Feuerstein ran out of money, and Malden Mills was forced to declare bankruptcy.

Welch, on the other hand, turned GE from a sleepy home-appliance company into an international mega-corporation that today is a leader in several industries. For every job he slashed, he eventually created dozens of new ones. For all the praise heaped on Feuerstein and scorn heaped on Welch, it is Welch, not Feuerstein, whose "coldhearted," capitalist management style did the most good for the most people.

> *A company that is seen as a good "corporate citizen" is a company more likely to win favor and patronage from members of the community.*

There's also a delicious twist in the tale. After its bankruptcy, Malden Mills was dangerously close to going out of business completely. Only the last minute heroics of a group of corporate lenders saved the company from going under. Want to guess who the chief stakeholder of those lenders was? It was GE Capital Corporation, a group that likely wouldn't exist were it not for the leadership of Jack Welch.

A corporation's only duty is to its shareholders. Corporations must abide by the law, of course. But a company that breaks the law and incurs the fines, bad press, and compensation that will follow is not acting in the interest of its shareholders.

Certainly, there's room for a large corporation to invest in its community, to sponsor local arts, education, and charity programs. But community investment plays into "ruthless profit-

2seeking" too. A company that is seen as a good "corporate citizen" is a company more likely to win favor and patronage from members of the community.

Today, anti-corporatists want corporations to put some vague notion of altruism ahead of profit, innovation, and investment. That's terribly shortsighted. Capitalism has proven to be the best way of creating wealth because it trusts that the collective wisdom millions of people voluntarily engaging in millions of mutually-beneficial transactions every day is the best way for an economy to allocate its resources.

When we're free to pursue what's best for us individuals, we inevitably create the kind of order and produce the wealth that is best for us as a society.

We need to get away from the notion that unfettered capitalism is amoral or, worse, *immoral*. As the Welch-Feuerstein example shows, if we define moral corporate practices as those practices which create the most good for the most people, "ruthless profiteering" is not only not incompatible with morality, it brings about a great deal more morality than altruism does.

11

Well-Funded Environmental Groups Abuse Their Power

John Perazzo

John Perazzo is a columnist and the author of The Myths That Divide Us: How Lies Have Poisoned American Race Relations.

The environmental movement is run by a small cadre of extremists who seek to undermine the capitalist system. Groups such as the Rainforest Action Network and Nature Conservancy promote an antibusiness agenda. Ironically, they rake in millions of dollars in revenues from their real estate holdings, stock portfolios, and business deals. They also get millions of dollars in grants from foundations such as the left-wing Ford Foundation. While the people who run environmental groups pose as grassroots advocates of nature, they pay themselves salaries that would make most CEOs envious. Moreover, their organizations make enormous profits by making emotional appeals about fuzzy animals and endangered insects. Americans must stop being fooled by the elite liberals behind the environmental movement who are mainly interested in enriching themselves while standing in the way of jobs and economic benefits for average citizens.

We have all seen the photos of cute, fuzzy creatures and flower-speckled hills adorning the Websites and promotional literature of America's leading environmentalist groups.

These groups portray themselves as grassroots organizations of ordinary nature-lovers motivated purely by a desire to preserve, for the welfare of future generations, those pristine areas of our nation's landscape not yet spoiled by the smoky breath of industrial pollution. But in truth, environmentalism's major objective has little to do with clean air, pure water, or cuddly wildlife. Rather, it is a vast network of radical leftist organizations dedicated to nothing less than the overthrow of American capitalism, which they deem the source of all environmental ills.

Almost all of today's environmentalist groups were created with grants from one or more elite foundations, among the most prominent being the Ford Foundation, which regularly funds leftist political causes.

Randall Hayes, president of the Rainforest Action Network, calls capitalism "an absurd economic system [that is] rapidly destroying nature." Greenpeace International puts it this way: "When the last tree is cut, the last river poisoned, and the last fish dead, we will discover that we can't eat money." Far from being a grassroots movement, almost all of today's environmentalist groups were created with grants from one or more elite foundations, among the most prominent being the Ford Foundation, which regularly funds leftist political causes. "Seed grants" from Ford and other foundations establish radical groups as new, independent entities that can thereafter commence their own fundraising operations under the pious banner of "environmentalism."

The environmentalist establishment is comprised of thousands of groups—some local, some national—but virtually all well funded and able to pursue a multitude of often-obscure issues. Many people wonder, for instance, what motivates such groups to jump on the particular bandwagons they choose, such as a California group organized solely for the purpose of protecting an obscure species of flies. The answer is simple: these groups understand that the allegedly threatened welfare of such an insect could provide the pretext needed to someday derail the construction of a proposed factory, housing development, corporate office building, or road slated for a particular location. To set the stage for this scheme, a leftwing foundation such as the Ford Foundation makes a grant to establish a group purportedly dedicated to protecting the species in question, and a cause is thus created. The nominal beneficiaries take many forms: spotted owls, snail darters, band-winged grasshoppers, moss spiders, beach mice, gray bats, and flatwoods salamanders, to name just a few. The "endangered species" list in the U.S. alone currently contains no fewer than 70 varieties of clams, 32 types of snails, 16 kinds of beetles, and 19 breeds of butterflies.

Environmental Protection Is Big Business

Contrary to the public image of an everyman's movement, environmentalism is in fact big business, raking in more than $8.5 billion per year. If we factor in the revenues of law firms involved in environmental litigation, this figure nearly doubles. Environmentalist group income is larger than the Gross National Product (GNP) of about five-dozen nations worldwide. No trade association on earth possesses the financial resources and political influence of the environmental lobby. There are more than 3,000 so-called nonprofit environmental groups in the U.S. today, most of which take in over $1 million annually. In one recent year, Greenpeace International took in $35 million, the National Audubon Society $79 million, the National Wildlife Federation $102 million, the Sierra Club $74 million, the Nature Conservancy $972 million, and the World Wildlife Fund $118 million. In addition, each of these groups holds assets ranging from $16.3 million to $2.9 billion.

Only a small portion of these immense revenues comes from the checkbooks of concerned individual donors. Much of the money comes from the groups' real estate holdings, product marketing, business deals, and huge stock portfolios. In other words, the very movement that condemns capitalism for allegedly ravaging the environment happily takes advantage of capitalism to rake in mounds of cash. Indeed, many environmentalist organizations buy stock in companies whose industries they consistently denounce as "harmful" to the environment: lumber companies, mining companies, and manufacturers of bulldozers and logging equipment such as Caterpillar and John Deere. Other environmentalist groups round out their portfolios with holdings in real estate, utilities, and government securities. The anti-capitalists further feed from capitalism's trough by accepting at least another $200 million per year in corporate donations.

The bigwigs of the environmental game are careful to save themselves an ample piece of capitalism's pie; environmental executives have average annual salaries in the $200,000 neighborhood.

Environmentalist groups also exploit their non-profit status and reputations as selfless wildlife protectors by buying and selling vast tracts of land. The Nature Conservancy (NC), for instance, buys real estate from landowners at a reduced cost and then sells it to the government for an inflated price. In one recent year, the NC bought and sold more than 73 million acres in this manner—all in the name of "saving the environment." Notably, environmentalist groups use a hefty portion of such windfalls only to feather their own financial nests with such things as luxurious new offices, high-profile lobbyists, high-priced economists and attorneys, and millions of direct-mail pleas for still more money. Moreover, the bigwigs of the environmental game are careful to save themselves an ample piece of capitalism's pie; environmental executives have average annual salaries in the $200,000 neighborhood.

Funding from the Ford Foundation

The rest of environmentalism's funding comes largely from prestigious foundations like the Ford Foundation. Each year, hundreds of foundations earmark thousands of grants totaling hundreds of millions of dollars for environmentalist groups. Many of these foundations are part of an informal coalition called the Environmental Grantmakers Association (EGA), comprised of more than 250 private donors responsible for most of the money given to such groups. The EGA holds private annual retreats to plan strategies for achieving its desired programs and policy outcomes—almost exclusively leftwing, anti-business, and anti-private property ownership. Occupying a prominent place at the EGA meetings is the Ford Foundation, which has a long history of donating enormous sums to environmentalist causes.

Depicting itself as a non-profit entity dedicated to fighting the capitalistic greed that purportedly ravages the environment, the tax-exempt [Natural Resources Defense Council] holds assets exceeding $71 million.

In 1969, for instance, a large Ford Foundation seed grant established the Washington, D.C.–based Environmental Defense Fund (EDF), a group that made its name in the early-1970s fight to ban DDT, the life-saving insecticide that was turning the tide on malaria. Among EDF's other achievements was its role in drafting California's first sweeping environmental regulations in the form of Proposition 65, the ballot initiative that restricted the use of many chemicals in industry and agriculture and has cost the California economy billions of dollars. The Ford Foundation has funded EDF heavily over the years, its generosity highlighted by a $500,000 grant in 1988, a $400,000 grant in 1996, and a $150,000 grant in 1998. Today EDF has seven offices nationwide, more than 150,000 members, and an annual operating budget of $17 million.

A $400,000 Ford Foundation seed grant in 1970 also established the Natural Resources Defense Council (NRDC), a radical leftist group that serves as one of the environmentalist movement's legal arms. The NRDC has filed dozens of lawsuits to block the construction of highways, hydroelectric dams, and nuclear power plants, but is perhaps best known for being the source of an enormous and costly apple industry hoax about Alar in 1989. Another NRDC signature issue is its fight to shut down the timber industry. Depicting itself as a non-profit entity dedicated to fighting the capitalistic greed that purportedly ravages the environment, the tax-exempt NRDC holds assets exceeding $71 million.

A very partial list of other Ford Foundation grants made in the past few years includes the following: $225,000 to the Wilderness Society, $200,000 to Friends of the Earth, $2 million to the Nature Conservancy, $48,000 to the World Resources Institute, $75,000 to the NRDC, $250,000 to the Environmental Law Institute, $225,000 to the Environmental Working Group, $50,000 to the National Environmental Trust, and $300,000 to the National Wildlife Federation. According to the Capital Research Center (CRC), which was established in 1984 to study non-profit organizations, all of the aforementioned organizations are politically far-left. Other recent Ford grants include: $150,000 to the American Land Institute, $500,000 to the Rainforest Alliance, $96,000 to the Center for Marine Conservation, $32,000 to the Conservation Fund, $150,000 to American Rivers, $100,000 to Northwest Environment Watch, and $400,000 to the Pratt Institute Centre for Community and Environmental Development.

Four years ago [in 2000], the Ford Foundation also gave $150,000 to the International Forum on Globalization (IFOG), a think-tank of some five-dozen anti-capitalist organizations with close ties to the Rainforest Action Network. IFOG founder and president Jerry Mander calls capitalism and economic globalization "the greatest single contributor to the massive ecological crises of our time," characterized by an "inherent emphasis on increased trade requir[ing] corresponding expansion of transportation infrastructures—airports, seaports, roads, rail-lines, pipelines, dams, electric grids—many of [which] are constructed in pristine landscapes, often on Indigenous people's lands. Increased transport also uses drastically increased fossil fuels, adding to the problems of climate change, ozone depletion, and ocean, air, and soil pollution."

That, in a nutshell, is the environmentalist view of capitalism. Therefore, the next time you hear an environmentalist group depicting itself as a grassroots enterprise of average Americans who spontaneously banded together to save the environment, remember that its true agenda is political, not environmental. Moreover, it is most likely an enormously wealthy entity funded by some of the deepest pockets on earth, such as those of the Ford Foundation.

12

The Greedy Practices of Corporations Are Destroying the Environment

Michael Parenti

Michael Parenti is a political analyst and an award-winning author of eighteen books. His most recent publications include Superpatriotism *and* The Assassination of Julius Caesar.

For the rich and powerful who run American industry, money is more important than the environment. With an overt hostility toward those who advocate saving the planet for future generations, these corporate CEOs have successfully lobbied the government to weaken a host of environmental regulations. Although global warming, water pollution, and tainted air will affect their children and families, these industrial plutocrats care only about short-term monetary gain. Unless environmentalists fight harder against this greedy minority, the desire of the industrialists to accumulate more wealth will serve only to doom the human race.

With its never-ending emphasis on production and profit, and its indifference to environment, transnational corporate capitalism appears determined to stand outside nature. The driving goal of the giant investment firms is to convert natural materials into commodities and commodities into profits, transforming living nature into vast accumulations of dead capital.

This capital accumulation process treats the planet's life-sustaining resources (arable land, groundwater, wetlands, forests, fisheries, ocean beds, rivers, air quality) as dispensable ingredients of limitless supply, to be consumed or toxified at will. Consequently, the support systems of the entire ecosphere—the Earth's thin skin of fresh air, water, and top soil—are at risk, threatened by global warming, massive erosion, and ozone depletion. An ever-expanding capitalism and a fragile finite ecology are on a calamitous collision course.

Utter Antagonism

It is not true that the ruling politico-economic interests are in a state of denial about this. Far worse than denial, they have shown utter antagonism toward those who think the planet is more important than corporate profits. So they defame environmentalists as "eco-terrorists," "EPA gestapo," "Earth Day alarmists," "tree huggers," and purveyors of "Green hysteria" and "liberal claptrap."

> The driving goal of the giant investment firms is to convert natural materials into commodities and commodities into profits, transforming living nature into vast accumulations of dead capital.

The plutocracy's position was summed up by that dangerous fool, erstwhile Senator Steve Symms (R-Idaho), who once said that if he had to choose between capitalism and ecology, he would choose capitalism. Symms seemed not to grasp that, absent a viable ecology, there will be no capitalism or any other ism.

In July 2005, President Bush finally muttered a grudging acknowledgment: "I recognize that the surface of the Earth is warmer and that an increase in greenhouse gases caused by humans is contributing to the problem." But this belated admission of a "problem" hardly makes up for Bush's many attacks against the environment.

Anti-Environment Measures

In recent years, Bushite reactionaries within the White House and Congress, fueled by corporate lobbyists, have supported measures to

1. allow unregulated toxic fill into lakes and harbors,
2. eliminate most of the wetland acreage that was to be set aside for a reserve,
3. completely deregulate the production of chlorofluorocarbons (CFCs) that deplete the ozone layer,
4. eviscerate clean water and clean air standards,
5. open the unspoiled Arctic wildlife refuge in Alaska to oil and gas drilling,
6. defund efforts to keep raw sewage out of rivers and away from beaches,
7. privatize and open national parks to commercial development,
8. give the remaining ancient forests over to unrestrained logging,
9. repeal the Endangered Species Act,
10. and allow mountain-top removal in mining that has transformed thousands of miles of streams and vast amounts of natural acreage into toxic wastelands.

A Different Reality

Why do rich and powerful interests take this seemingly suicidal anti-environmental route? We can understand why they might want to destroy public housing, public education, Social Security, and Medicaid. They and their children will not thereby be deprived of a thing, having more than sufficient private means to procure whatever services they need for themselves.

But the environment is a different story. Do not wealthy reactionaries and their corporate lobbyists inhabit the same polluted planet as everyone else, eat the same chemicalized food, and breathe the same toxified air?

In fact, they do not live exactly as everyone else. They experience a different class reality, often residing in places where the air is somewhat better than in low and middle income areas. They have access to food that is organically raised and specially prepared. The nation's toxic dumps and freeways usually are not situated in or near their swanky neighborhoods. The pesticide sprays are not poured over their trees and gardens. Clearcutting does not desolate their ranches, estates, and vacation spots.

The plutocrats deny there is a serious problem because they themselves have created that problem and owe so much of their wealth to it.

Even when they or their children succumb to a dread disease like cancer, they do not link the tragedy to environmental factors—though scientists now believe that present-day cancer epidemics stem largely from human-made causes. The plutocrats deny there is a serious problem because they themselves have created that problem and owe so much of their wealth to it.

But how can they deny the threat of an ecological apocalypse brought on by ozone depletion, global warming, disappearing top soil, and dying oceans? Do the corporate plutocrats want to see life on Earth—including their own lives—destroyed?

Pollution Pays

In the long run they indeed will be sealing their own doom, along with everyone else's. However, like us all, they live not in the long run but in the here and now. What is at stake for them is something more immediate than global ecology. It is global capital accumulation. The fate of the biosphere seems a far-off abstraction compared to the fate of one's immediate investments.

Furthermore, pollution pays, while ecology costs. Every dollar a company spends on environmental protections is one less dollar in earnings. It is more profitable to treat the environment like a septic tank, to externalize corporate diseconomies by dumping raw industrial effluent into the atmosphere, rivers, and bays, turning waterways into open sewers.

Moving away from fossil fuels and toward solar, wind, and tidal energy could help avert ecological disaster, but six of the world's ten top industrial corporations are involved primarily in the production of oil, gasoline, and motor vehicles. Fossil fuel pollution means billions in profits. Ecologically sustainable forms of production directly threaten those profits. Immense and imminent gain for oneself is a far more compelling consideration than a diffuse loss shared by the general public. The social cost of turning a forest into a wasteland weighs little against the personal profit that comes from harvesting the timber.

We Don't Think of the Long Term

This conflict between immediate personal gain on the one hand and seemingly remote public benefit on the other operates even at the individual consumer level. Thus, it is in one's long term interest not to operate an automobile that contributes more to environmental devastation than any other single consumer item (even if it's a hybrid).

But again, we don't live in the long run, we live in the here and now, and we have an immediate everyday need for transportation, so most of us have no choice except to own and use automobiles.

Mind you, we did not choose this "car culture." Ecologically efficient and less costly mass transit systems and rail systems were deliberately bought out, privatized and torn up, beginning in the 1930s in campaigns waged across the country by the automotive, oil, and tire industries. These industries put "America on wheels," in order to maximize profits for themselves, and to hell with the environment.

The plutocrats are more wedded to their wealth than to the Earth upon which they live, more concerned with the fate of their fortunes than with the fate of humanity.

Sober business heads refuse to get caught up in doomsayer "hysteria" about ecology. Besides, there can always be found a few stray experts who will obligingly argue that the jury is still out, that there is no conclusive proof to support the alarmists. Conclusive proof in this case would come only when the eco-apocalypse is upon us. Ecology is profoundly subversive of capitalism. It needs planned, environmentally sustainable production rather than the rapacious unregulated free-market kind. It requires economical consumption rather than an artificially stimulated, ever-expanding, wasteful consumerism. It calls for natural, relatively clean and low cost energy systems rather than high cost, high profit, polluting ones. Ecology's implications for capitalism are too challenging for the capitalist to contemplate.

The plutocrats are more wedded to their wealth than to the Earth upon which they live, more concerned with the fate of their fortunes than with the fate of humanity.

The struggle over environmentalism is part of the class struggle itself, a fact that seems to have escaped many environmentalists. The present ecological crisis has been created by the few at the expense of the many. This time the plutocratic drive to "accumulate, accumulate, accumulate" may take all of us down, once and forever.

13

Wealthy Corporations Unfairly Influence News Coverage

Peter Hart and Julie Hollar

Peter Hart is in charge of media activism for FAIR, a national media watchdog group. Julie Hollar is FAIR's communications director.

Most Americans learn about current events from television, newspapers, and magazines. Media owners and corporations therefore have extraordinary powers to control the political and cultural dialogue in the United States and, unfortunately, often use their influence to promote their own interests. For example, media conglomerates use their influence to publicize the books, TV shows, movies, and magazines they produce. In addition, some corporate advertisers pressure news outlets to promote their products in news stories. With CEOs wielding a powerful influence over the media, the news is tainted with barely disguised ads and entertainment gossip. Worse, some media corporations are pressured by corporate advertisers not to run disturbing news reports because the contrast between sobering news and light-hearted commercials is so great. In a time of war, terrorism, and natural disaster, journalists and editors must take the high ground and resist pressures to slant the news to benefit a wealthy few.

We can get five reporters a month to do news stories about your product. If you want to be interviewed by 10 to 20 re-

porters per month, we can arrange that, too. . . . Media Relations, Inc. has placed tens of thousands of news stories on
behalf of more than 1,000 clients.

—Media Relations, Inc. solicitation

The PR [public relations] agency's promises are a stark reminder that the news is, in many ways, a collision of different interests. The traditional tenets of journalism are challenged and undermined by other factors: Advertisers demand
"friendly copy," while other commercial interests work to
place news items that serve the same function as advertising.
Media owners exert pressure to promote the parent company's
self-interest. Powerful local and national interests demand
softball treatment. And government power is exerted to craft
stories, influence content—and even to make up phony "news"
that can be passed off as the real thing.

---

*Journalists "report more cases of advertisers and owners
breaching the independence of the newsroom."*

Journalists, on the whole, understand these pressures all
too well. A survey of media workers by four industry labor
unions found respondents concerned about "pressure from
advertisers trying to shape coverage" as well as "outside control of editorial policy." In May [2004] the Pew Research Center for the People & the Press released a survey of media professionals that found reporters concerned about how bottom-
line pressures were affecting news quality and integrity. In
their summary of the report, Bill Kovach, Tom Rosensteil and
Amy Mitchell wrote that journalists "report more cases of advertisers and owners breaching the independence of the newsroom."

The Fear & Favor report [of *FAIR* magazine] is an attempt
to illustrate this growing encroachment on journalism with
real examples that have been made public—not an exhaustive
list by any means, but a reminder that such pressures exist,

and that reporters serve the best interests of citizens and the journalistic profession by coming forward with their own accounts.

In Advertisers We Trust

USA Today served notice that corporate advertisers have a remarkable influence over what we see on the TV screen. As the paper noted, in the media world "there is worry that the flood of grisly images flowing into living rooms from Iraq and elsewhere will discourage advertisers."

A General Motors spokesperson explained that her company "would not advertise on a TV program [just] about atrocities in Iraq," while an ad exec explained that "you don't want to run a humorous commercial next to horrific images and stories." A Ford representative said the company keeps a close eye on news images that accompany its ads, saying, "We're monitoring the content and will make decisions based on the nature of the content. But we don't have a lot of control."

> *When a super-sized corporation comes to town . . . newspapers sometimes seem more than willing to suspend the rules of critical journalism to ingratiate themselves with the wealthy new arrival.*

But they do, of course. Commercial media wouldn't exist without, well, the commercials. And in order to keep the revenue flowing, media outlets increasingly blur the lines between their advertising and editorial divisions.

When a super-sized corporation comes to town, it brings along an ad budget to match, and newspapers sometimes seem more than willing to suspend the rules of critical journalism to ingratiate themselves with the wealthy new arrival. When furniture giant Ikea opened a new store in New Haven, Connecticut, the *New Haven Register* cranked out 12 Ikea stories in eight straight days—accompanied by at least 17 photo-graphs and a sidebar on product information—with headlines such as "Ikea's Focus on Child Labor Issues Reflects Ethic of Social Responsibility" and "Ikea Employees Take Pride in Level of Responsibility Company Affords Them." The *Register's* Ikea reporter was even sent to Sweden to visit the company's head-quarters—on Ikea's dime, according to *Columbia Journalism Review*, a little detail the *Register* failed to disclose.

People in powerful positions have long pulled strings to influence news coverage, with journalists sometimes act-ing as witting accomplices.

The back-scratching reached its apex the day of the grand opening, when the *Register* heralded the arrival of Ikea and fellow super-store Wal-Mart and remarked upon Ikea's "aston-ishingly low prices—a coffee table for $99, a flowing watering can for $1.99, a woven rocking chair, $59." Sound like an ad? It was the *Register's* lead *editorial . . . .*

Powerful Players and PR

It's not just advertisers who have the clout to bend the rules of journalism. People in powerful positions have long pulled strings to influence news coverage, with journalists sometimes acting as witting accomplices. When a journalist at *Bloomberg News* filed a report about a civil suit against Deutsche Bank [in 2004] it didn't seem like a particularly remarkable story; a former female employee was accusing the company of firing her for complaining about, among other things, sexual harass-ment by Damian Kissane, a former Deutsche Bank exec. But to the surprise of the newsroom staff, editor-in-chief Matthew Winkler had it purged from the Bloomberg website and re-placed six days later with a bowdlerized version that deleted the names of all parties involved. Shortly afterwards, he issued a memo to the staff, admonishing that *Bloomberg News* "must never be a mouthpiece for litigants who want to publish court filings to embarrass or gain an advantage over their opponents."

Winkler claimed the story "lacked context" and a sense of "why do we care about this." The *New York Post* reported that Kissane, now Chief Operating Officer of the financial markets branch of the Royal Bank of Scotland, was said to have complained to Winkler. Bloomberg insiders cited by the *New York Post* suggested that Winkler rewrote the story in response to Kissane's complaint—perhaps unsurprisingly, since Bloomberg's main business is selling market information to the financial industry. . . .

The Boss' Business

When conservatives complained that CBS was promoting [President George W.] Bush critic Richard Clarke on *60 Minutes* without disclosing that his book *Against All Enemies* was published by Free Press, another Viacom subsidiary, CBS responded by saying that the show "has interviewed authors from virtually all the book publishing companies over its 36 seasons and is beholden to none of them. Publishers seek out *60 Minutes* because it is television's No. 1 newsmagazine." But the question is not whether authors wouldn't want to get on *60 Minutes* if they didn't work for the same company; the question is, are we really supposed to believe they don't get preferential consideration when they do?

As a [2004] report in the *American Journalism Review* [*AJR*] noted, comments filed with the FCC [Federal Communications Commission] regarding its ownership regulations provided some concrete examples that such mutual back-scratching does go on. *AJR* quoted a newspaper reporter whose bosses also owned a TV station:

> When the Nielsen TV ratings come out, I know I am expected to write a big story if the co-owned station's ratings are good and to bury the story if the co-owned station's rat-

ings are down. Or another example. A few years ago, I ran a survey asking readers what they thought of local television news programs. My general manager told me the next time I do something that might affect our sister station, I better check with him first. I got the message. I haven't done a similar project since then.

The violation of the boundary between news and entertainment is perhaps nowhere as flagrant as on network "news-magazine" shows. As a May 14 [2005] *Los Angeles Times* story explained, the NBC News program *Dateline* found plenty of news value in the entertainment offerings of NBC. "Despite criticism that NBC's news programs have been turned into brazen marketing tools for several of the network's prime-time series finales," the *Times* reported, "the management of the combined company seems delighted with the promotional firepower of its enterprise." The *Times* cited, among other things, the two-hour *Dateline* devoted to the final episode of the sitcom *Friends,* as well as generous coverage of the NBC sitcom *Frasier* and the Donald Trump "reality" show *The Apprentice.*

Thanks to NBC's recent acquisition of Universal, network news president Neal Shapiro looks forward to NBC's news programs getting first crack at interviewing movie stars affiliated with Universal films. He dismissed criticisms of this blurring of the lines between news and entertainment as "asinine.". . .

More Examples of Self-Promotion

During the May "sweeps" period (when advertising rates are set based on audience share), *TV Guide* counted over 117 minutes of NBC promotions on the *Today* show. CBS's *Early Show,* which runs an hour less than *Today,* finished second with just over 107 minutes. ABC's *Good Morning America* came in last with just under 36 minutes of self-promotion. Former morning show producer Steve Friedman told the magazine that "it's inevitable that a morning show or a magazine show will do these segments," adding: "You'd be a fool not to do it. It's a business."

Washington Post TV reporter Lisa de Moraes catalogued the self-promotion she found in just that day's listings. ABC's *20/20* profiled reality TV star Victoria Gotti, whose *Growing Up Gotti* program just happened to be airing on the A&E cable channel—owned by ABC parent Disney. Over at CBS, the *48 Hours* newsmagazine profiled Yoanna House, who lost 60 pounds to try out for *America's Next Top Model,* a reality show airing on the UPN network—which, like CBS, is owned by Viacom. De Moraes pointedly remarked: "Remember how the broadcast networks explained that they would cover only three hours of each of the four-day Democratic and Republican conventions because they are nothing more than infomercials out of which no real news comes?"

The network that pays for the rights to broadcast the Olympic Games always happens to find the Olympics far more newsworthy than its network competitors. In 2004, according to the *Tyndall Report's* tally of network newscast coverage, *NBC Nightly News* devoted 106 minutes of news time to the Athens events; by comparison, ABC dedicated 34 minutes of news time, and CBS only 15. NBC executive producer Tom Touchet, who works on the *Today* show, felt no conflict, telling the *Atlanta Journal Constitution* that "his bosses haven't asked him to do anything he wasn't comfortable with."

On July 9, ABC's *20/20* presented a segment on the legend of King Arthur. While that might be an odd topic for a newsmagazine show, even more unusual was one of the guest "experts" chosen to share his views on the subject: Hollywood bigwig Jerry Bruckheimer, whose "expertise" consisted in being the producer of the new Disney film *King Arthur.* As the *Christian Science Monitor* noted, "If the weakness of Bruckheimer's grasp of Arthurian lore was obvious, the connection between his movie and ABC television wasn't. Only at the end of the segment did the reporter mention that Disney owns ABC."

As the *Monitor* explained, Disney/ABC felt no need to even conjure up a good explanation for the decision: "The movie producer was included in the show for business reasons, not because he was the most knowledgeable source, acknowledges David Westin, president of ABC News. 'It made good sense for us, frankly,' he says, 'to take advantage of all the marketing and publicity for the movie.'"

14

America's Wealthiest Citizens Give Away Billions to Improve Education

Richard Lee Colvin

Richard Lee Colvin is director of the Hechinger Institute on Education and the Media, based at Teachers College, Columbia University.

The richest and most powerful people in the United States are also among the most generous. Billionaires such as Microsoft Corporation founder Bill Gates and GAP clothing chain founder Donald Fischer give away billions of dollars to fund school construction, teacher training, curricula development, and other worthy educational causes. Using the same creative skills they used to build their fortunes, this new generation of donors has set out to create a revolution in charitable giving by taking a hands-on approach to philanthropy, becoming personally involved in their charitable projects. The new philanthropists have donated so much money to public schools that nearly everyone in education is benefiting.

Last February [2005], in a speech in Washington, D.C. that drew 45 of the nation's governors as well as a hefty sample of the nation's education policy elite, Microsoft chairman Bill Gates issued a jeremiad on the state of the American high school, arguing that this venerable institution is obsolete and a threat to the nation's economic and political well-being. Declarations that public education in general and high schools in particular turn out badly prepared graduates, perpetuate inequities, and generally operate in ways that run counter to the nation's interests have become almost commonplace. But coming from Gates, whose prodigious wealth and aggressive tactics have become one of the nation's best-known narratives of entrepreneurship, the words took on new meaning. Stories in the *New York Times, Los Angeles Times, Washington Post,* and many other newspapers, most written not by education reporters but by Washington-based political and legislative correspondents, reported Gates's assertions in an unquestioning, almost awestruck tone that made one thing clear: if high schools are bad enough for Bill Gates to declare them a disaster, then it must be so.

It was publicity that even the world's richest man could not buy.

But Gates's standing to speak authoritatively on the issue rested on more than his wealth, celebrity, and business acumen, or even his company's need to hire well-trained workers. Through the efforts of his richly endowed Bill & Melinda Gates Foundation, Gates has become an unparalleled force who is not only sounding the alarm about America's high schools, but is also putting forth, and financing, a range of specific solutions. Since 2002, the Gates Foundation has allocated more than $1.2 billion toward creating about 820 new high schools and breaking down about 750 large, comprehensive high schools into smaller, more focused, more intimate academies that aim to send far more students off to college prepared to succeed. The foundation is also the lead partner in a $125 million experiment in "early college" high schools, which are designed to enable 9th graders to get their high-school diplomas as well as two years of college credit, all within four or five years. To increase the impact of its initiatives, the Gates Foundation has involved 13 other foundations and is working with more than one hundred intermediary organizations in two hundred cities located in almost every state. The foundation's goal is ambitious: to improve the national graduation rate to at least 80 percent, from about 65 percent, while increasing the likelihood that all high-school graduates are college-ready. So, more spending, in more places, is likely on the way.

The Money Pours In

American philanthropy, by local and national foundations, corporations, and wealthy individuals, has played many important roles in K–12 education: creating new schools, underwriting research, funding scholarships, testing hypotheses, generating new curricula, invoking ideals, setting agendas, bolstering training, and building a case for policy changes. Foundation money is so widespread, and so sought after, that few in education are unaffected. . . .

> American philanthropy, by local and national foundations, corporations, and wealthy individuals, has played many important roles in K–12 education.

Even though some foundations have reduced their involvement in K–12 education or shifted their education investment to prekindergarten or afterschool programs, far more philanthropists are entering the scene than are leaving, says Bill Porter, executive director of Grantmakers for Education.

Indeed, according to the Future of Philanthropy project, an analysis done by a Cambridge, Massachusetts, consulting group, the number of foundations involved in education is expected to swell. Over the next two decades, Americans will pass on to their heirs huge sums, approximately $1.7 trillion of which will go to charities and to endow foundations. And, typically, about 25 percent of philanthropic dollars goes to education, although more goes to higher education than to elementary and secondary schools. Gates, just to use one example, has a personal net worth estimated by *Forbes* magazine to be $46 billion, and he has vowed to give away 95 percent of his assets during his lifetime.

The New Philanthropists

Plenty of other heavyweights in the world of business are contributing heavily to education causes already. They include Jim Barksdale, the former chief operating officer of Netscape, who gave $100 million to establish an institute to improve reading instruction in Mississippi; Eli Broad, the home builder and retirement investment titan, whose foundation works on a range of management, governance, and leadership issues; Michael Dell, the founder of Dell Computers, whose family foundation is valued at $1.2 billion and is a major supporter of a program that boosts college going among students of potential but middling accomplishment; financier and buyout specialist Theodore J. Forstmann, who gave $50 million of his own money to help poor kids attend private schools; David Packard, a former classics professor who also is a scion of one of the founders of Hewlett-Packard and has given $75 million to help California school districts improve reading instruction; and the Walton Family Foundation, which benefits from the fortune of the founder of Wal-Mart, and which is the nation's largest supporter of charter schools and private school scholarships.

As is clear from this partial list, many of the newcomers are in the West, or otherwise far from the old-money power centers of the East. A number of the individual donors did not come from money, but attended public schools before amassing their fortunes. As a group, they share a belief that public education has not done well by immigrants or poor students, hardly a radical claim. But they are less likely than were donors in the past to think that the solution to that problem lies solely or even primarily in spending more money or even in making the allocation of resources more equitable, which has been a common thread in work that many better-established foundations have pursued.

The San Francisco–based Pisces Foundation, for example, was endowed by Donald Fisher, founder and chairman emeritus of the Gap clothing chain, and his wife, Doris. By 2005 Pisces was the biggest single supporter of Teach for America, a nonprofit that has, improbably, made teaching in poverty-ridden urban schools one of the most popular career choices of students at Ivy League colleges. Pisces also gave about $35 million to fund the national expansion of the instructionally demanding Knowledge Is Power Program charter schools, which serve mostly low-income students. Overall, the foundation is spending about $20 million a year to "leverage change in public education—especially in schools serving disadvantaged students—through large strategic investments in a small number of initiatives that bolster student achievement." That rate of spending was about the same as that of the venerable Carnegie Corporation and would have put the foundation in the top ten or so givers to K–12 in 2002.

Many are personally involved in overseeing the grants they give and they insist on results from educators and schools.

Like Fisher, other new philanthropists tend to believe that schools, in addition to securing adequate financial resources, need to embrace accountability and to overhaul basic functions. Many are personally involved in overseeing the grants they give and they insist on results from educators and schools. They believe good leadership, effective management, compensation based on performance, competition, the targeting of resources, and accountability for results can all pay dividends for education as well as for foundations. They tend to set ambitious goals for their own work and to be aggressive in pursuit of their agendas. That, too, is something of a departure for philanthropists, who have tended to stay in the background and let their grantees set their own goals while they bask in the spotlight.

"These are people who made money challenging the status quo," says Barry Munitz, president and CEO of the J. Paul Getty Trust, referring to the new givers. "These high net worth, first-generation folks . . . approach their gift-giving the way they approached their investing—due diligence, measures of accountability, a lot of involvement, each with an agenda. It's very different from spending money on the system and standing back and letting it work." . . .

Leadership, Management, and Governance

By the end of 2004, the education foundation established by Eli Broad and his wife, Edythe, had assets worth $540 million. The foundation has already committed some $135 million to overhauling fundamental aspects of urban school districts: identifying new sources of talent for positions of authority; developing alternative training methods for managers, principals, and teachers union leaders; creating new tools for analyzing performance data; and working with school boards to help those sometimes obstructionist bodies become more focused on student learning than on petty power plays. Broad, whose fortune is variously estimated at between $4 billion and $6 billion, is in his 70s, and he too plans on giving away most of that amount during his lifetime. Most of it will go toward K–12 education causes, according to Dan Katzir, the education foundation's managing director.

The foundation supports a number of what Katzir calls "branded flagship initiatives," such as the Broad Center for the Management of School Systems or the Broad Institute for School Boards. Its largest investment is a $20 million-plus stake in SchoolMatters.com, a project of Standard & Poor's

School Evaluation Services unit that marries information about how schools spend their money with academic indicators.

Another major foundation that has invested heavily—even more so than Broad—in improving the skills of principals and superintendents is the Wallace Foundation, which was established by DeWitt and Lila Acheson Wallace, the founders of the Reader's Digest Association. In 2000 the foundation committed $150 million over five years to improving leadership at the school and district level and is now underwriting in 24 states a wide variety of programs: leadership academies, university-school district partnerships, research, changes in what it takes to become certified as a principal, and superintendent training. Wallace and Broad, as well as Annenberg and Gates, also are underwriting the New York City Leadership Academy, a very expensive undertaking that pays aspiring principals full salaries as they train for a year to take jobs heading up schools in the city.

The Wallace Foundation's Richard Laine emphasizes that it is not enough just to improve the training of principals. Put a well-trained leader in a bad system, he's fond of saying, and "The system will win every time." What's needed, he says, are policy changes, giving the best teachers incentives to go into the most demanding schools and allowing principals to have more control over hiring and evaluating teachers and more flexibility and control over their budgets.

Teaching

Improving teaching has long been high on the agenda of many foundations. "It really all boils down to good teaching," says Janice Petrovich of the Ford Foundation. "If you can figure out how to do that, you'll make a difference."

That, however, turns out to be difficult for foundations to do well and even more difficult to sustain. Foundations actively working on this front today have a wide variety of strat-

egies for making a difference. Some of these might be catego-
rized as efforts to build the capacity of the current system by
simply paying for professional development sessions on particular topics; others might be thought of as attempts to
change the system by developing new approaches to hiring,
compensating, and evaluating teachers. Ultimately, Petrovich
says, increasing the capacity of the system changes the system.
But foundations often are reluctant to work inside classrooms
to help teachers, for fear that they won't have a systemic impact; at the same time, to make a difference broadly, foundations have to fund projects over which they have little control.

---

*The Milken Family Foundation has spent well over $100
million to make teaching more attractive.*

One of the most ambitious efforts to improve teaching is
called Teachers for a New Era, a $65 million project under-
written by four venerable foundations: Carnegie, which initi-
ated the effort and has the largest stake; Annenberg; Ford; and
the Rockefeller Foundation. As of 2003, 11 education schools
had received five-year grants to develop teacher-preparation
programs that mimic the kind of clinical training that doctors
receive as residents and that pay more explicit attention to the
effect of the training on student learning. The grants must be
matched locally.

The Milken Family Foundation has spent well over $100
million to make teaching more attractive by recognizing
achievement and pushing districts to base pay on performance. The foundation's Teacher Advancement Program,
which provides training opportunities to help teachers climb a
career ladder toward higher salaries based on their performance, is now in place in 85 schools and is poised for a major
expansion, with states and the federal government offering financial support.

"We are hell-bent on figuring out a way of creating the proper incentives and putting them into practice to attract talented people into the profession," Lowell Milken says.

Another foundation committed to improving teaching is the William and Flora Hewlett Foundation, where Marshall Smith, a former acting deputy secretary of education in the Clinton administration, heads up education reforms. The former dean of the Stanford University School of Education, Smith is perhaps the leading proponent of what's known as "systemic" reform in education. He says that about half of the $36 million or so he has to spend on K–12 education annually goes to "trying to figure out ways of improving instruction in inner-city schools."

Academic content and performance standards are now well ingrained in American public education, Smith believes. But the standards movement that he had a hand in launching "really doesn't touch the classroom in a deep way. What's arisen in the past five or six years as an issue is the quality of the teacher and whether we have the capacity and smarts and knowledge to improve that."

15

Most Rich Americans Have Worked Hard to Obtain Their Wealth

B.Z. Khasru

B.Z. Khasru is a journalist and managing editor of the Westchester County Business Journal.

The richest people in the United States often labor long hours in order to obtain wealth. While a few have achieved overnight success from start-up Internet companies, most millionaires have become rich by dedicating themselves to hard work over a protracted period of time. This practice has allowed a large percentage of America's most affluent people to reach the top after starting life in the lower or middle classes. Contrary to the popular notion that most affluent people inherit their wealth, a good percentage have become rich through sacrifice, hard work, and a commitment to their jobs.

For a few lucky Americans, the Internet superhighway may have offered a short road to wealth, but most people take more than two decades to finish the road to financial success.

In fact, the top 1 percent of America's wealthy—with an annual adjusted gross income of $300,000 or a net worth of more than $3.75 million—worked for 21 years on average to attain their current financial status, according to a study.

B.Z. Khasru, "Road to Wealth Paved with Hard Work, Sacrifice," *Westchester County Business Journal*, vol. 41, July 22, 2002, pp. 2–3. Copyright © 2002 by Westfair Communications, Inc. Reproduced by permission.

They worked an average 48 hours a week, and among respondents who work full time, nearly one-third work more than 50 hours weekly, according to the latest U.S. Trust Survey of Affluent Americans.

People do not necessarily become rich through inheritance. Only 5 percent rated inheritance as a "very important source of their wealth." More than two-thirds described "their childhood economic situation as poor, lower class or middle class," but a majority of them today consider themselves as "upper class," and more than one-third consider themselves "wealthy."

Hard Work and Good Investments

For many Americans, the corporate world remains the top source of wealth, with 41 percent saying they gained their fortunes through corporate employment, followed closely by earnings from a private business (37 percent) or a professional practice (36 percent) and through securities investments (33 percent). One-quarter consider real estate as an important source of wealth.

The study, based on interviews with 150 households nationwide, found that 89 percent believe "willingness to work hard" is a "very important factor" to achieve financial success, 71 percent think "ability to get along with others" is a very important factor, and 69 percent attribute the success to "professional or technical skills."

The top 1 percent of America's wealthy . . . worked for 21 years on average to attain their current financial status.

Martin S. Berger, chairman of City and Suburban Bank in Yonkers, considers himself among America's top 1 percent in terms of wealth. He agrees with the findings.

"In my opinion, it's hard work, good luck and conservatism in investment philosophy," he said, adding good luck essentially relates to understanding when to invest and when to withdraw from the market—whether putting money in stocks or real estate. This wisdom comes with experience and time, he said.

Berger and his partner, Robert Weinberg, are among the top three investors of Mack-Cali Realty Corp., a real estate investment trust. Berger said he gained his fortunes in a matter of 10 years by investing in home building and apartment construction after his discharge from the Air Force in 1955 when he was 25 years old.

No Time for Family

Darien, Conn., resident Robert Dilenschneider, founder of The Dilenschneider Group, a corporate strategic public relations counseling firm in New York City, said one must work hard to be rich.

"People who are wealthy probably forego some of the pleasures of life in order to gain wealth."

"People who are wealthy work 80 or 90 hours a week," said the author of several best-selling books, including "Power and Influence." "They don't put in 35 hours a week. People who are wealthy probably forego some of the pleasures of life in order to gain wealth."

"Some of the rich people do not have time to pay attention even to their children because they are so busy making money," he said.

William R. Berkley, chairman of W.R. Berkley Corp., an insurance company in Greenwich, Conn., considers himself a wealthy person.

"Nothing can replace hard work, but the difference between hard work and earning a living is understanding how to leverage your work," he said.

"You can get paid for your hard work, but how you leverage your skills in every way—how you charge people, how to motivate people to work for you, how you bring a good idea to fruition with the help of other people—all ensure extra mileage out of one's hard work," he said.

Berkley said he was surprised to learn that most people surveyed had to work 71 years on average to gain their financial freedom. "In today's world, it would be faster than that," he said. "I would have said 15 years. But one thing is sure. It does not happen overnight, no matter how much you try."

How long did it take Berkley to become rich?

"It took me a lot less than 15 years," he said.

Contrary to the popular notion, educational background and mentoring are considered less significant factors for financial success—a finding that did not surprise Dilenschneider.

"Many of the people who graduated top of their class did not do well," he said. "People like [billionaire] Donald Trump did not graduate high of their class. You have to be able to get along with other people and be able to adjust to the world around you" to be successful in life.

Organizations to Contact

Americans for Tax Reform (ATR)
1920 L St. NW, Suite 200, Washington, DC 20036
(202) 785-0266 • fax: (202) 785-0261
e-mail: friends@atr.org
Web site: www.atr.org

ATR opposes all tax increases in the belief that a system should exist in which taxes are simpler, fairer, flatter, more visible, and lower than they are today. Members believe that the government's power to control one's life derives from its power to tax and that that power should be minimized. ATR publishes press releases, editorials, and the *Tax Reformer* newsletter.

Cato Institute
1000 Massachusetts Ave. NW
   Washington, DC 20001-5403
(202) 842-0200 • fax: (202) 842-3490
email: jblock@cato.org
Web site: www.cato.org/index.html

The Cato Institute is a nonprofit libertarian public policy research foundation headquartered in Washington, D.C. The institute seeks to broaden the parameters of public policy debate to allow consideration of the traditional American principles of limited government, individual liberty, free markets, and peace. The institute researches issues in the media and provides commentary for editorials in magazines, newspapers, and news programs.

Center for American Progress
805 Fifteenth St. NW, Suite 400
   Washington, DC 20005
(202) 682-1611

e-mail: kcooper@amprog.org
Web site: www.centerforamericanprogress.org

The Center for American Progress is a research and educational institute dedicated to promoting progressive viewpoints on issues such as media bias, income disparity, national security, the economy, and the environment. The center's daily publication *Progress Report*, available by e-mail, analyzes the media and questions viewpoints perceived to be biased toward conservative policies in the news.

The Center for Responsive Politics
1101 Fourteenth St. NW, Suite 1030
  Washington, DC 20005-5635
(202) 857-0044 • fax: (202) 857-7809
e-mail: info@crp.org
Web site: www.opensecrets.org

The Center for Responsive Politics is a nonpartisan, nonprofit research group based in Washington, D.C., that tracks money in politics and its effect on elections and public policy. The center conducts computer-based research on campaign finance issues for the news media, academics, activists, and the public at large. Its work is aimed at creating a more educated voter, an involved citizenry, and a more responsive government. The organization publishes position papers, documents that track paybacks for political patronage, and the *Capital Eye*, a newsletter that examines the role of money in the U.S. political system.

Center for the Defense of Free Enterprise
12500 NE Tenth Pl., Bellevue, WA 98005
(425) 455-5038 • fax: (425) 451-3959
Web site: www.cdfe.org

The Center for the Defense of Free Enterprise was founded by a group of businessmen, educators, legislators, and students who were deeply concerned about the multitude of restrictions being imposed on America's free enterprise system by big government—and the lack of understanding of this problem by the American people. The organization publishes a variety of position papers available on its Web site.

Fairness and Accuracy in Reporting (FAIR)
112 W. Twenty-seventh St., New York, NY 10001
(212) 633-6700 • fax: (212) 727-7668
e-mail: fair@fair.org
Web site: www.fair.org

FAIR is a national media watch group that documents media bias and censorship. The organization advocates for greater diversity in the press and scrutinizes media practices. FAIR publishes a bimonthly magazine, *EXTRA!*, that analyzes media treatment of important issues and points out perceived conservative bias.

Hudson Institute
1015 Eighteenth St. NW, Suite 300
  Washington, DC 20036
(202) 223-7770 • fax: (202) 223-8537
e-mail: info@hudsondc.org
Web site: www.hudson.org

The Hudson Institute is a conservative think tank that supplies research, books, and policy ideas to leaders in communities, businesses, nonprofit organizations, and governments. The institute is committed to free markets and individual responsibility, confidence in the power of technology to assist progress, respect for the importance of culture and religion in human affairs, and determination to preserve America's national security.

Inequality.org
220 Fifth Ave., 5th Floor, New York, NY 10001
(212) 633-1405
Web site: www.inequality.org

The mission of Inequality.org is to illuminate the causes and consequences of America's growing concentration of wealth, income, power, and opportunity and to move the neglected problem onto the front burner of American politics and public discourse. The group publishes books, such as *Inequality Matters: The Growing Economic Divide in America and Its Poisonous Consequences*, along with commentary and policy papers available on its Web site.

OMB Watch
1742 Connecticut Ave. NW
   Washington, DC 20009
(202) 234-8494 • fax: (200) 234-8584
e-mail: ombwatch@ombwatch.org
Web site: www.ombwatch.org

OMB Watch is a nonprofit research and advocacy organization dedicated to lifting the veil of secrecy shrouding the powerful White House Office of Management and Budget (OMB). OMB Watch promotes government accountability, citizen participation in public policy decisions, and the use of fiscal and regulatory policy to serve the public interest. OMB Watch publishes the biweekly newsletter *Watcher* and issues reports, guides, and annual/biennial organization reports available electronically for free download.

Public Citizen
215 Pennsylvania Ave. SE
   Washington, DC 20003
(202) 546-4996 • fax: (202) 547-7392
e-mail: cmep@citizen.org
Web site: www.citizen.org/cmep

Public Citizen is a national, nonprofit consumer advocacy organization founded in 1971 to represent consumer interests in Congress, the executive branch, and the courts. Public Citizen fights for openness and democratic accountability in government; for the right of consumers to seek redress in the courts; for clean, safe, and sustainable energy sources; for social and economic justice in trade policies; for strong health, safety, and environmental protections; and for safe, effective, and affordable prescription drugs and health care.

United for a Fair Economy (UFE)
29 Winter St., Boston, MA 02108
(617) 423-2148 • fax: (617) 423-0191
e-mail: info@faireconomy.org
Web site: www.faireconomy.org

United for a Fair Economy is a national, nonpartisan organization founded to raise awareness about the issue of concentrated wealth and power, which UFE believes undermines the economy, corrupts democracy, deepens the racial divide, and tears communities apart. UFE publishes books such as *The Wealth Inequality Reader* and *Greed and Good: Understanding and Overcoming the Inequality That Limits Our Lives*. Reports, opinion pieces, and policy papers are available on its Web site.

Bibliography

Books

Gar Alperovitz — *America Beyond Capitalism: Reclaiming Our Wealth, Our Liberty, and Our Democracy*. Hoboken, NJ: J. Wiley, 2005.

Benjamin F. Bobo — *Rich Country, Poor Country: The Multinational as Change Agent*. Westport, CT: Praeger, 2005.

W. Michael Cox and Richard Alm — *Myths of Rich & Poor: Why We're Better Off than We Think*. New York: Basic Books, 1999.

Richard B. Freeman — *The New Inequality: Creating Solutions for Poor America*. Boston: Beacon, 1999.

Martin S. Fridson — *How to Be a Billionaire: Proven Strategies from the Titans of Wealth*. New York: Wiley, 2000.

Daniel M. Friedenberg — *Sold to the Highest Bidder: The Presidency from Dwight D. Eisenhower to George W. Bush*. Amherst, NY: Prometheus, 2001.

Brian L. Goff — *Spoiled Rotten: Affluence, Anxiety, and Social Decay in America*. Boulder, CO: Westview, 1999.

Mark Victor Hansen — *Cracking the Millionaire Code: Your Key to Enlightened Wealth*. New York: Harmony, 2005.

Arianna Huffington	*Pigs at the Trough: How Corporate Greed and Political Corruption Are Undermining America.* New York: Crown, 2003.
Gary Indiana	*Schwarzenegger Syndrome: Politics and Celebrity in the Age of Contempt.* New York: New Press, 2005.
Robert A. Isaak	*The Globalization Gap: How the Rich Get Richer and the Poor Get Left Further Behind.* Upper Saddle River, NJ: Prentice-Hall/Financial Times, 2005.
David C. Johnston	*Perfectly Legal: The Covert Campaign to Rig Our Tax System to Benefit the Super Rich—and Cheat Everybody Else.* New York: Portfolio, 2003.
Lewis H. Lapham	*Lapham's Rules of Influence: A Careerist's Guide to Success, Status, and Self-Congratulation.* New York: Random House, 1999.
Robert L. Nadeau	*The Wealth of Nature: How Mainstream Economics Has Failed the Environment.* New York: Columbia University Press, 2003.
Benjamin I. Page and James R. Simmons	*What Government Can Do: Dealing with Poverty and Inequality.* Chicago: University of Chicago Press, 2000.
Dick Pels	*Media and the Restyling of Politics: Consumerism, Celebrity, and Cynicism.* London: Sage, 2003.
Sam Pizzigati	*Greed and Good: Understanding and Overcoming the Inequality That Limits Our Lives.* New York: Apex, 2004.

Lee Rainwater and Timothy M. Smeeding
Poor Kids in a Rich Country: America's Children in Comparative Perspective. New York: Russell Sage, 2003.

Martin Ravallion
A Poverty-Inequality Trade-Off? Washington, DC: World Bank, Development Research Group, Poverty Team, 2005.

Jeffrey Reiman
The Rich Get Richer and the Poor Get Prison: Ideology, Class, and Criminal Justice. Boston: Allyn and Bacon, 2001.

Alan Schroeder
Celebrity-in-Chief: How Show Business Took Over the White House. Boulder, CO: Westview, 2004.

Roy C. Smith
The Wealth Creators: The Rise of Today's Rich and Super-Rich. New York: Truman Talley/St. Martin's, 2001.

Alissa J. Stern
The Process of Business/Environmental Collaborations: Partnering for Sustainability. Westport, CT: Quorum, 2000.

Daniel M. West and John M. Orman
Celebrity Politics. Paramus, NJ: Prentice-Hall, 2002.

Liesbet van Zoonen
Entertaining the Citizen: When Politics and Popular Culture Converge. Lanham, MD: Rowman & Littlefield, 2005.

Periodicals

Mark Battersby
"More Wealthy Americans Aren't

Paying Taxes," *Investment News*,
July 18, 2005.

Jared Bernstein   "The Hierarchy: Income Inequality in
the United States," *Multinational
Monitor*, May 2003.

Nick Bromell   "Show Them the Money," *Harper's
Magazine*, May 2000.

Jonathan Chait   "For Richer—Conservatives v. Capitalism," *New Republic*, October 29,
2001.

Jeremy
Greenwood   "The Third Industrial Revolution:
Technology, Productivity, and Income
Inequality," *Economic Review*, Spring
1999.

Heidi Hartmann   "Closing the Gap Amidst Ongoing
Discrimination: Women and Eco-
nomic Disparities," *Multinational
Monitor*, May 2003.

John Lynch et al.   "Income Inequality, the Psychosocial
Environment, and Health: Compari-
sons of Wealthy Nations," *Lancet*, July
21, 2001.

Fred Magdoff and   "Disposable Workers: Today's Reserve
Harry Magdoff   Army of Labor," *Monthly Review*,
April 2004.

Rosemarie
Maldonado   "Rich Intent on Keeping What They
Have Now," *Investment News*, Sep-
tember 17, 2001.

Robert W.
McChesney   "Waging the Media Battle," *American
Prospect*, July 2004.

Robert McIntyre — "A Taxing Problem: Diminishing Progressivity in the U.S. Tax System," *Multinational Monitor*, May 2003.

Brigid McMenamin — "Home Free: Wealthy Americans Renouncing US Citizenship to Avoid Paying Taxes," *Forbes*, July 26, 1999.

Dan Moldea and David Corn — "Influence Peddling, Bush Style: When Democrats Took Money from Wealthy Asians, It Was Called a Fundraising Scandal. When Members of the Bush Family Do It, It's Called Business," *Nation*, October 23, 2000.

Jan Narveson — "We Don't Owe Them a Thing! A Tough-Minded but Soft-Hearted View of Aid to the Faraway Needy," *Monist*, July 2003.

Andrew Stephen — "Land of the Free, Home of the Stingy: Americans, Who Think They Are Uniquely Generous, Give Just Five Cents a Day Each to Charities Abroad," *New Statesman*, January 10, 2005.

Edward Wolff — "The Wealth Divide: The Growing Gap in the United States Between the Rich and the Rest," *Multinational Monitor*, May 2003.

Index